ON THE ROAD

WITH RAMA

Rama - Dr. Frederick Lenz

LIVING FLOW

Contents

CHAPTER ONE

NEUTRAL DENSITY

Today I'd like to talk to you about neutral density—the neutral density of perpetual being—being awareness without being aware of yourself as such.

It's February 6th, 1985. I'm at around 9,000 feet. Pulled off at the side of the road, surrounded by snow, at a power place in the mountains of Colorado, up in the area of the Continental Divide. Every once in a while, a car whizzes past and then disappears around the bend as if it had never been.

The neutral density of being is the acceptance of your own immortality, your awareness of awareness.

One of the problems that you will probably come up against in self-discovery at a certain point, or maybe at several repetitive times, is role-playing.

Now, role-playing is something that you encounter first when you begin to meditate, when you begin to learn about awareness in new ways and you see or realize that you've been playing a series of roles all your life, that the world is not what it appears to be and that we've been taught to perceive in specific ways.

Each of these methods of perception, or perceptual modalities, defines life.

Our parents give us a series of them. Our school system, books we read, television programs, our encounters with other children growing up or with adults, experiences we have within our own mind, feeling our body perceptions—desires, pain, sensations of comfort and discomfort—all of these things paint a description for us of the world.

But as we learn in self-discovery, the world is not, of course, what it appears to be.

The world is awareness, endless awareness.

And there are rings of awareness, circles of awareness that we enter into for a period of time. You'll experience a type of awareness, a circle of awareness, and then pass on to another and to another.

As small children the circle of our awareness is an open circle. It's not a binding circle. It's not something that stays with us all of the time. It's a circle that leads to other circles—

> the numinous ring of awareness.

But as we appear to grow older the circles become constricting; they're binding.

The circle of awareness is closed.

We can't seem to get around to the other side without going back to where we've been. Everything's the same wherever we go. It isn't—life isn't—the feeling that you've perceived this before, that you've just made love and it was like the other 500 times, that you've just eaten dinner and it was like so many forgotten dinners, that you've just met someone and they're just another person, you've meditated and it was [just] another meditation.

In nature we tend to open ourselves, the circle opens a little bit because there's no mind in nature.

It's the mind, the circle of the mind, the circle of ideas that causes us to believe.

And these beliefs eventually permutate into an interlocking system of awarenesses, which is a role.

Each person plays a role and the role becomes more defined as they grow older.

Now by role, I don't simply mean father or mother, sister, brother, wife, husband, lover, soldier, scientist, cut-throat, good person, bad person, rich person, poor person, Indian chief.

By role, I mean not so much a socially defined structural way of being

> but the actual method of perception that you employ
> to look at yourself—

> how you think of yourself,

> how you think of yourself not simply as you define
> yourself in relation to the rest of the world,

> but how you define the world in relation to yourself.

You see life according to your awareness.

> Everything you see is a reflection of your awareness.

Life isn't really a specific way. It's an endless series of rings that we step in and step out of. Each ring has certain parameters and permutations. Each ring houses awarenesses.

> So if I'm in a specific ring and it's a ring of emotion,
> then everything I see will be colored by emotion.
> Everything will move me to a passion, a love, an

anger, a disquiet, sorrow, a rapture.

If I'm in the ring of mysticism, everything I'll see will be imbued with power. Everything will be a manifestation of power. I'll look at a rock and I'll see the type of power that it has. I'll look at a tree and see its living power. Everything will be power.

If I'm in the ring of spirituality, everything will be in the realm of light and stillness. And each thing will have a gradient of stillness, a quotient of light. And that light I will see as a reflection of a universal light, an endless light that is perpetual being, which is God.

In the ring of religion, I'll relegate all things to higher powers and think of myself as someone who's insignificant, who's not particularly capable, but only by the grace of God, some extension—which we call love, the grace of God—I exist, I breathe, I live, I have being, and I will owe my allegiance to that.

If I'm not necessarily religiously oriented but I'm oriented more in the direction of the pure experience of the cosmos without the terminology, then everything will be nirvana, perpetual being—not a sense of God as person or object or thing or even objective correlative of awareness, my awareness—undifferentiated reality. No beginning. No middle. No end. Beyond comprehension, beyond knowledge, yet containing both knowledge and ignorance in all things yet not bound by them.

Each ring promises us something. But the rings turn inside on us. In the beginning when you start to meditate, you'll see that you've been playing a role all your life.

You've been playacting.

But the role you've been playing has very little to do with yourself, which is why you're not particularly happy [and] why the energy—the kundalini—doesn't flow through you very well.

Some people refer to the inability for the kundalini to flow through someone as "blockages," as if there are specific places in the subtle physical body where there's some sort of a dam and the kundalini can pass no further.

> It's really not like that. There are actually places where the kundalini does rest. But the blockages are not in the subtle physical body.
>
> Rather, the blockages are awareness rings that we put around ourselves to keep the totality of existence at arm's length.

There's the sense of not being able to deal with everything, with all of eternity, all of its vastness, its complexity.

So we build a wall around ourselves, a ring of power. This wall is very much like the dikes that they built in Holland to keep the water out—this vast ocean is all around and if we don't have those dikes, the ocean will just flood us and sweep us away and destroy us.

So we build a dike and the purpose of the dike is to keep chaos—that which is beyond the human form and understanding—away from us and to create a defined area, a sense of definition—the land as opposed to the water—where human life can exist.

Everyone has that ring. To not have that ring is to be enlightened or insane—

> insane, suggesting that a person is in so many different realities that they can't quite catch up with themselves and so they've lost the command of the totality of their being;
>
> enlightened, meaning that a person is in so many realities that they've found themselves and that they are in the command of the totality of their being.

To simply push yourself forward into the unknown, to stretch your awareness endlessly, to just push your mind and your consciousness into the infinite awareness

> does not necessarily engender enlightenment
>
> because consciousness is very fragile and
>
> you are made up of a matrix of awareness, of
>
> very sensitive lines of light that are your being.

And to just throw those awarenesses into that vast cosmos at random can be destructive, in the sense that the fragile organism that you are will be destroyed.

> You will merge back into the totality of absolute being.
>
> It's a type of death.

Enlightenment is different than that. Enlightenment is "seeded awareness."

We plant a seed and it sprouts and grows, and it grows from this world into other worlds and from those worlds into eternity itself. But there's a sense of growth and development of harmony—the same type of harmony we see reflected in the organic life of plants, in human beings and animals and all structures.

So the role that we play—the role that you play, that you grew up playing, that formed around you—

> was initially there to provide a sense of self, a sense of being,

so that if you're at a traffic light in your car, you're not so out there in perpetual being that when the light changes color you'll have no sense of what color it is or what a car is or what you're doing there—

the ability to function in the first level of attention,

the world of time and space, to be here now, in the moment, aware of the moment but not bound by the moment as an idea, to create a description of life that enables you to walk through this world and enjoy it,

> but not a description that's so tight that it constricts you
>
> and prevents you from realizing God—eternal awareness—the beauty, the plain old beauty of the moment, of now, this second of your life, which is forever.

So in the early stages of self-discovery you go through a lot of changes. As you're meditating, as the kundalini begins to circulate a little bit, you begin to break out of the stratified awareness that you've had all of your life. The ring that binds you falls away.

And you quickly pick up another ring. It's a habit that we have. It's like a snail that abandons its shell to seek another shell. It doesn't want to be outside of its shell for very long because it's very vulnerable.

So here we are. You're listening, I'm talking. I'm at around 9,000 feet and the energy is different here.

The forces are different up here in the Continental Divide, or whenever you reach a very high altitude.

As I'm talking, some of them are gathering around the car; I can see them.

These are beings that live up here because they like it, because the vibratory energies of the Earth are radically different at different altitudes.

A great sense of the commotion of the world, the *fwif* and *fwam,* the noise, the thoughts, the thought forms of human beings, which are powerful in their own right, don't really reach up this high. And even if someone is up here thinking them, they don't have the power to overcome the neutral density of this area.

You see, the United States is divided into power zones.

That is to say, the eastern part of the country on the eastern side of the Continental Divide is one power sector.

The lines of energy, the magnetic lines of energy, run in specific directions and they run in almost the opposite direction on the western side of the Continental Divide.

The Divide itself is the point where the energy meets. It's like two rivers merging—at the point of merging there's a great deal of activity.

The sunset—it's neither dark nor light—and the sunrise, are the moments of transition.

And moments of transition are a time when the ring of our awareness falls away for a moment and we can see eternity more clearly.

So for me to be here in this moment is to be aware of you, to sense you, to feel who, in what you would call the future, will be listening to my voice—to feel each one of you because the future already exists.

It's just a ring of awareness. And I step into that ring for a moment so that I can be with you now.

Not with a sense of knowing that Joe or Suzie is listening, but feeling your being—because what's in a name anyway?

But also to be aware of the beings that are around my car, that are standing here hovering, vibrating, forms of energy and light, drawn by the energy of my body, my awareness. And I celebrate life with them as I'm drawn up here by the energy of their bodies.

Together we're all part of creation. And they have a ring of awareness as I look at them now and describe them to you—sort of our on-the-spot, man-on-the-spot reportage, Walter Cronkite at the Continental Divide with the astral beings. "Good evening ladies and gentlemen,"—that sort of thing.

And they're most beautiful, they're most luminous, the ones that are here now. They have many shapes and sometimes their shape changes constantly. It's not necessarily fixed. All kinds of colors. It's just most beautiful. Some are more powerful than others. Some are funny. Some don't have feelings like you do. No emotions. They hover in worlds of power, of energy. Others are extremely aesthetic. Some are forms that were once human and now they've transmuted into something else and have never been part of the human cycle or bardo.

I lead an interesting life.

So the description that you have falls away. It gradually disappears as you meditate and you adopt a new description, which is the description of the world of meditation and self-discovery—different terms and phrases denoting levels of consciousness, planes of attention. The methodologies of self-discovery.

And this ring doesn't bind quite as tightly. It's freer because its very essence suggests that it's only a ring.

But it's easy to get confused again and create another description, which is the egotistical description of self-discovery in which there's the apprehension—in other words, you think and feel—that you know more than somebody else. You know more than the waitress who's serving you coffee just because you can go into some other dimensional planes. Big deal. She's in other dimensional planes all the time; she just doesn't know it. We all are. Everyone is everything anyway.

So the spiritual elitism takes over and there's a sense of superiority, or a sense of goodness takes over.

If you have to choose between one and the other, choose a sense of goodness. But that can be just as binding.

The idea is that suddenly you're going to become very good, and let's say you actually do. You have a set idea of what goodness is and you manage to achieve it—a rare accomplishment unless you have a pretty loose idea.

Now you're good. [Rama chuckles.] Now what are you going to do? You're stuck with goodness. You're in more of a mess than you ever figured because now that you've become successful at being good, you've got to be good all the time. What a drag! You are good. Wonderful.

But you're not. That's one aspect of your being. But you're many more things than just good.

So now if you're going to be good and be good all the time and be good for everyone—you're totally selfless, humble, kind, considerate—all of the wonderful qualities. If you've managed to polish the stone of the self till it shines and you reach that point, that's a great achievement.

And now you're stuck. You're happy, yes. But you're stuck. Because there's a force within you, that kundalini, that wants to break out even beyond goodness, beyond happiness, beyond knowledge.

And that's to be something that can't be perceived by the mind, to follow a road that doesn't have a destination.

There's no sense as you walk along this road of going anyplace or having been anyplace because this road changes constantly. It's not a road that leads through the hills and you can walk on the road today and tomorrow you'll walk on it and see the same things.

It's simply not like that. This is a road that changes every moment. Thousands of realities come in and out of it. In one step you can go through a thousand shifts of attention.

And you can't ever take that step again. You can turn around and what you saw behind you before is gone; now turn back to where you just were and there's something else there. You look at yourself and it's someone else—continuous permutations of the self—not one ring but many.

Now of course, inside the ring there's nothing, and outside the ring there's nothing.

> The ring is the idea that you hold of yourself.

So the thought then, oh nobly born, is to be very, very careful

> of not being who you are.

And the litmus test, the way you can tell that it's happening to you, is very simple.

If after you've been meditating for a year or two or more you begin to find that you're not quite having as much fun with your meditation—your life does not seem to be quite as revolutionary, the Che Guevara element is lacking, you're not taking your machete of discrimination and hacking down the weeds of knowledge and logic, the should be, have been, was, I will be, prepositions, adverbs, conjunctions, interjections, grammatical forms slashed away; pronouns, pronomeal adverbs slashed away until there's nothing left—no language, no form, no description, no discussion, no sanity, no insanity—alive, feeling, wondering, shifting, changing, lost, found.

If it's not like that, it's getting dull.

And you should do something about it!

But what are you going to do?

[Rama talks in the tone of a whimpering person] "You're so good now, it's terrible, I'm so sorry for you. Oh gosh, Suzie, what are you going to do? You're stuck and there's no way out. You're good and you know it."

[Rama talks in the tone of an icily stern person] "And you've let everybody else know it and they're all walking around hating you because you're good. They can feel your goodness and they loathe your goodness" [back to normal voice] because everybody knows you're not really completely good.

Because goodness is just another idea, it's another abstraction. And you're stuck and you're a pompous ass; even though you're good, you can be a pompous ass.

Take it from one who's been there.

Goodness is disgusting. So is its opposite. So then, what's a mother to do? I mean what can you do in a situation like this?

You're up here in the Continental Divide and the beings are zooming around you and the sun is setting and the snow is everywhere. And at the same time you're with someone in some distant future who's listening to your voice, understanding exactly what they're going through.

Well, what you can do is offer hope.

See?

Noah's out there and it rained a lot. He's out there. He's got all these animals on the ark, right? So he takes a bird. He says, "Listen, dove, go out there and, you know, see if you can find anything out there." The bird goes out there and cruises around.

He comes back with a McDonald's wrapper and they know they're safe. There's a McDonald's out there. The waters have receded and they're doing good business. [Rama laughs.] So you want to be enlightened, hey? Are you willing to pay the price?

The doorway is everywhere and the price is your life.

Everything in it, every moment, every state of attention, everything that you are, everything that you dream—and being willing to throw it away constantly—all your self-importance, all your knowledge, all your ignorance, all your ideas.

And of course, the further you get in your self-discovery and the more wonderful you are, and the more you know the spiritual books and you read them, and after a while it's actually getting boring reading the *Bhagavad-Gita* or *The Way Of Life* or whatever it may be, because you've read it so many times.

How could you have ever read it before since you never even existed until this second as this current form? If you're reading it again—dull, dull, dull!

Same old meditations? Same old kundalini? Same old tantra? Dull, dull, dull!

What are you going to do to break it up?

You've got to start over and be a perpetual beginner. That's the safest—to be a perpetual beginner, to find yourself a newness, to define yourself as newness, to run up the flag and walk away and leave and let it be on its own.

To leave everyone you know, and more importantly, to leave everyone who knows you.

We are prisoners of the thoughts of others. Thoughts have power.

Your friends, your loved ones, those who love you, those who could care less but who know you, who you've been too accessible to, you've let them inside your life.

[Rama talks in the tone of a whimpering person] "You've shared your emotions, your good feelings. Oh gosh, you're so swell." [Back to normal voice.] You've just let everybody see your pantyhose. How wonderful.

And now everybody knows all there is to know about you or about the ring that you're bound in, and they can apply pressure to it on various sides. They can hold you in your thoughts.

Your own ideas when shared with others become your undoing, in a sense, because then after awhile, they see you the way you see yourself and they hold that image in their thoughts and minds, and they apply it and it becomes stronger. It strangles you.

Leave everybody you know. Don't see them. Anyone who knows you absolutely well, leave them. Oh, you may see them, but leave them.

Inside, let go.

See people who don't know you well and don't do it again.

Become a mystery to yourself because if you know what you're going to do tomorrow, if you know how you're going to make the bed, if you know the kinds of clothes that you'll buy the next time you go shopping and you definitely know what you won't buy, if you think yourself beautiful or unbeautiful, if you are wed or unwed, if all these things are so apparent, then you are so stuck in a boring life.

And everywhere you turn you see reflections of your own boredom.

Life is never boring. Only you are boring.

You are boring because you don't live dangerously. You're not willing to live in eternal attention.

You're too lazy. You're not lazy. Look how much energy you have to do all the things that you do. You've never been lazy. No one's lazy. What we would call the laziest person on earth expends a tremendous amount of energy to not do things. So there are no excuses except the ones that are boring.

Everything is life. Everything is energy. Everything is consciousness.

So you've got to let go.

And stop playing a role, even now that you may have adopted a good role—this is what I'm suggesting.

We broke out of the old ones. Wonderful. And now we've all been meditating together for some years and we've got new roles. I'm a spiritual teacher. You're a spiritual aspirant. And the role of the spiritual teacher can be as deadly a trap as the role of spiritual aspirant. The role of the enlightened one can be as much of a trap.

And you say, "Well how can, how can, how can?" I don't know, but it can be. Who says it can't be? Who says anything is anyway, anyhow? Who are these people who keep telling us everything is this way or that way? Who wrote all those books? How do you know they're right? Have you experienced it yourself?

Why can't something be and not be at the same time? I see it all the time. I live in a world of constant, changeless, endless confusion. It's wonderful—the redolent disorder of life, which is perpetual, perfect being. Uniform nirvana. No measurements. No sizes. Nothing ever comes in the mail any more. The box is gone. Nirvana. No address. No forwarding. No zip code. No cellular phones.

So the key to all of this then would seem to be to develop a wonderful sense of humor and a reverence for life. And that's really about all you need.

That sense of humor keeps you meditating in new ways, and to meditate is to live. Life is meditation. It keeps you changing because you can look at yourself and realize, in all your spiritual advancement or in all your new discovery, how silly you are.

As you hold up your achievements and measure them against eternity, you know they don't show. Candle to the stars.

Where are you anyway? How did you get here? Why were you born? What is the meaning of life?

Are you in balance? What is your balance? Are you balancing yourself against some arbitrary standard or description?—is my point.

Or are you like, you know, uh gosh man, are you, uh, geez, are you making it up as you go along?

That's the way to do it. Just make it up as you go along. Because it isn't really ... the script isn't written.

You just have to get creative and break away from everyone who knows you and everything you know. You know about yourself so well. You know your reactions, your loves, your rights, your wrongs, your ins, your outs. Gee. [Rama laughs.]

But what good is it doing you! What good is it doing you? Are you seeing the rainbows of life still? Have you merged with the stillness? What good is it all doing you?

Don't hold on to these wonderful things. They're not so wonderful.

My judo teacher used to explain that whenever you grab someone and hold them to throw them, at the moment you do that, of course, you've just put yourself in a perfect position to be thrown. Because once you're holding on, that point of pressure, that point of attachment, can be used for your own demise.

So you should be very selective as to what you grab on to, and know that the circuit always runs two ways.

Life is perpetual beauty. Try not to grab on to too many things.

Remember that outside of time, outside of space, outside of duality, which are just ideas—and even the idea of the ideas themselves is just another idea—but still, there is something.

And that something is wonderful. Absolutely wonderful beyond understanding and that is the universe, the eternal universe. It's not just stars, planets, quasars, black holes and McDonald's hamburger stands.

It's endless light. It's awareness.

The universe is actually alive. It's intelligence—an intelligence that so far surpasses anything that has yet been seen or dreamed or imagined, and you enter into that intelligence. You are it. You're a reflection of it.

But to see it all, to be it, to be that totality, that's what attracts a few of us to perpetually go forward into it.

And it's neither moral nor amoral, good nor bad. It's not an achievement. It's just what you're drawn to.

We're drawn back to the sea of eternity, and along the way, there are places you can get stuck.

You're going down the river of life and there are little sandbars you can get your boat hung up on.

Or if you choose, you can stop at any point and get off the boat and walk around and see things. Then you get back. You know, it's Huck Finn and Jim headed down that Mississippi River, seeing life. Going into one town and having an experience. Getting back on the boat.

And they're happiest on that boat, cruising down the river looking up at the stars at night.

But then again, part of us always wants to get off and to see and experience different sides of life ... because everything we see is what we are.

So be careful of the trap of selfhood, be it the ultra-boring mundane selfhood, or the selfhood of goodness, the selfhood of spiritual awareness and achievement.

Be neither attracted nor repulsed, nor nebulous, nor advanced.

Beyond all these ideas and goals is perpetual beauty. To know that is to be free. And to be free of that is to know much more.

That which appears to be empty is full, and that which is full is never empty.

To meditate is easy. Stop your thoughts. Don't try and meditate in a specific way. Any way will do, and use any way. But don't try too hard.

Look beyond the thoughts, between them. Listen to the sounds around yourself.

Sit, close your eyes, keep the back straight, be

comfortable and listen.

The birds are singing. The cars are passing by. Life is passing us by.

Listen.

Don't listen to your mind talking, no matter what it says.

It's just a ring that keeps revolving around and you won't hear anything you haven't heard. It's an old tape played all too often. We've worn it out.

Listen to the silence and allow yourself to expand into it.

Don't worry about how.

Something will show you.

A light spirit will come to you and show you.

Something's leading you right now. It always has been. You've sensed it all your life. Trust the force—it will always be with you. Trust. Trust life.

Meditate each day for an hour or two or three, whatever's comfortable, and be absorbed.

And you'll grow to love those silent moments—those silent eternities, as you will dissolve in and out of the clear light of reality. You'll merge with all that has been, all that will be. You'll be the play of existence, and you'll see your thoughts parading before you sometimes—your frustrations, your desires. Be neither attracted nor repulsed.

Wave at them as they go by—go ahead, wave. Wish them well on their journey.

But know that you are not of them, and you are not in them.

They were just a ring that formed for a while, and after a while you believed that the ring was part of your own being, part of your own flesh. Let them go. A new ring will form. Then let that go—and so on and so forth.

Stepping from ring to ring, from wonder into wonder, existence opens.[1]

Meditate. Don't think too well of yourself nor too poorly. Help out those you can without thinking that you're too helpful. Avoid the trap of goodness.

And avoid the trap of being trapped, of thinking that you're trapped because that's just an idea. You're not trapped. You're living energy.

You're perpetual perfect being, you wonderful thing you! God, it's disgusting. I can't even be around you. You're so ecstatic!

Let go more. Hold on less. What's there to hold on to anyway? Remember when you hold on, you get thrown—an interesting experience.

Don't tell everyone what you do, what you feel, what you think, what you wear.

Just be, and you will find what you've always known is there.

The light of eternity will be your constant companion. Perpetual being. Heck, you can do it. Of course you can. Others have done it before you without trying very hard.

It's not necessarily hard to be enlightened. It's just hard not to be a jerk, that's all.

---

1. "From wonder into wonder, existence opens." from *The Way of Life,* by Lao Tzu, trans.Witter Bynner.

It's hard not to get stuck in your ideas of how horrible you are or how wonderful you are. You're not either. You're neither horrible nor wonderful.

You're a being of light composed of cells of light all joined together in a matrix.

And it's neither good nor bad. These ideas that zip through your mind are just formations of energy, ways of seeing yourself—they're rings. But they're not you.

Come now. Let's not be so unsophisticated. I mean spiritual chic is just knowing that you're clear light, and of course you want to be chic.

To think that you're good or bad, or moral or immoral, [Rama talks in the tone of a person whimpering] "I'm a failure. I can't do it. I can't meditate." [Rama talks in the tone of a happy person] "I'm so good."

Or, [Rama returns to whimpering tone] "I have to work so hard for others all the time because they just, they need me. They need me out there because I'm gonna save the world, and I'm good. I'm so good."

[Back to normal voice.] This is trash in the sense that it's boring. It's not chic. It's not hip.

Spiritual chic, [Rama laughs] what is it? It's to be free, of course! It's to be free! Who wants to be stuck in being religious and being spiritual either?

That's not freedom. You've just exchanged handcuffs for leg irons—which doesn't mean that you should avoid enlightenment.

Enlightenment has nothing to do with being spiritual.

Being spiritual is just an idea—it's another ring.

So is being occult, being powerful. It's all the same.

Frogs are jumping back and forth in the pond. It's snowing. The sun is setting. The reeds are growing. People are dying. People are being born.

No way. I don't believe it for a second.

There's only freedom. Being alive.

Don't worry about your future lives, past lives. Button your shirt. Stand up straight. Go out and do something. Go out and have some fun. Be alive, change, dissolve, explode. Touch life and be touched by it. But don't grab it because you'll be grabbed by it. And life can really grab you.

And when you die, at the moment of your death, remember that we once had a conversation. You had a friend—from another world—who dropped by to say that there is a pathway that does lead between the worlds.

Now as the sun goes over the mountain here and we enter that twilight time, there is a path that does lead beyond birth and death, and to go beyond birth and death, actually, you go through it.

It's a very interesting path. It changes without any sense of it changing because there's no such idea, I suppose. It just is. When the totality is the totality then there's no totality.

And the friend, anyway, the friend came by and said, "Look, so you die, big deal. You're not really dying. You're just stepping out of the bound circle for a while. Just keep going and don't look back."

Just keep going. Don't look back. Remember what happened to

Orpheus. Don't look back.

Once you get out of here, don't look back. Don't worry. Something will guide you. But if you look back, you'll come back.

You know, as you leave Sodom and Gomorrah, right, don't look back. Remember what happened to Lot's wife? Salt city. [Rama laughs.]

Don't look back. We're told again and again in varying ways, don't look back. Keep going. Keep going. I'll see you there. I'll be waiting for you at that big McDonald's in the sky where all the burgers are made of soy and the fries are never greasy.

Nirvana. Never a cover charge.

See you there. Good luck.

CHAPTER TWO

UNITY

Today is March 30th. It's around 5 o'clock in the afternoon. I'm on the Big Island of Hawaii, and I'm pulled off to the side of the road at around three thousand feet. I'm going to roll up the window here 'cause it's getting a little loud.

There's a lot of traffic on this particular road, but it's a power place. Beneath me I see the island stretching out. The sun will probably be setting in about an hour. I'm facing the direction of the volcano Mauna Kea. It's obscured by a heavy cloud cover. Behind me is Mauna Loa—the twin peaks of the Big Island.

And today I'd like to talk to you about making yourself available to energy, to power.

You've decided to look for power, to look for light, to look for truth. So now you've started on your journey. But there are some things that you need to consider. The first is to be strategic. The second is to be earnest, and the third is not to give a damn. They really all go together.

What is power anyway? What is energy? What is light? What is the thing that we seek? It's awareness.

Awareness is everything. Our awareness shapes the world. And if you control awareness, you control the world.

Awareness is not just the sense of seeing in time. Awareness is the very fabric that existence is made up of.

People have varying degrees of awareness depending upon their level of evolution—what they've done in their other lifetimes, how much of that has come forward, how much of that is still being held within. They have awareness of the world as it has been taught to them.

Everybody sees life in their own terms. Our awareness is colored, of course, by moods, mood swings, emotions, feelings—feeling good, feeling bad emotionally. The body colors our awareness, the body awareness—pleasure, pain, sickness, health, fatigue, feeling energetic. Awareness, of course, is very, very influenced by our desires. We desire to become something, we desire to have something or we desire to avoid something. Awareness is modified by all these things.

But what is awareness? Aside from all these modifications, what is it that is aware in us? Who is it who is listening to this tape? Who is it who is speaking these words? Does the world exist without us? What is the "us"? It's awareness.

Awareness is really not a simple thing. It's very, very complex. As we progress through life, we move through different states of attention, different states of awareness.

And we, in a sense, become those states of attention. When you were five or six or seven years old, you had a certain state of awareness or attention, and that for you was the whole world. That was your world. Everything that you experienced and felt was modified.

Awareness is the screen on which the movie of life is projected.

Awareness is also the viewer.

Now, here's an interesting point. Awareness becomes aware of itself. Awareness perceives itself, but not always completely. Awareness can think of itself, feel itself, speculate about itself, correctly or incorrectly. It depends on what level or gradient of awareness we're dealing with.

You're aware. You're aware that you're seeking power, you're seeking energy. And it's been my experience as one who has sought awareness and continues to do so, that in the beginning, at least, awareness is something that appears to be outside of us.

We have the sense that we will be aware when we have traveled, when we have experienced something, when we've met someone, when we've interacted with something or someone.

But awareness really is within. Not within the body, certainly—it's within itself. Awareness is itself. And the way into awareness, well, it's the way into anything and everything, since anything and everything is awareness.

Did you know that everything has awareness? Rocks have awareness. Plants have awareness. Both sentient and insentient forms of beings, both living and what we would call non-living—everything is pulsing energy, pulsing life. But what we see is not all there is. There's a curtain that needs to be parted, and that is the curtain of temporal awareness.

Temporal awareness is the awareness of time and space. Or we could say it's the awareness that perceives that there is time and space, that there's matter and that there's energy, that there's yesterday, today and tomorrow. That's temporal awareness.

Eternal awareness is nirvana, of course.

Eternal awareness means nothing—no way to express it—that which would conceive or perceive of anything is washed away in the clear light of reality, in nirvana.

So nirvana really doesn't have awareness as we know it.

Nirvana's almost a misnomer in the sense that as soon as we hear a word, as soon as we name it, we get an idea as to what it must be like or not like. And that confuses everything.

The awareness that you have right now—how did it come to be? Where did it come from? Are you happy with it? Would you like to modify it, change it, shift it around? If you're listening, I assume that you want to modify it and shift it—for variety, if nothing else, if not for truth, for power, to become what you're capable of being, to be the sun and beyond the sun, to be the moon and beyond the moon. To be all. Yet all awareness is not really meant for human beings.

Think of it in terms of rings of power, rings of awareness.

The first ring of awareness is the ring of temporal awareness.

Now actually, when we're born, this ring doesn't exist yet.

When we first come into the world, we're in a second ring, what I refer to as the second attention—a very fluid awareness that has no boundaries.

The baby isn't aware of forward and back or inside and out. Yet it is awareness—pure, undifferentiated awareness, in a way.

But the baby's awareness is conditioned by experience. Heat, cold, sensations, comfort, discomfort, love, anger, the energies it feels around different people modify that baby's awareness.

Language, customs, traditions, social values, everything that we're taught modifies the awareness and creates a second ring of awareness, which is the first attention.

That's temporal awareness.

The first attention is intended to aid us in life. It protects us. It enables us to cross the street, make a business decision, pick out a card for somebody's birthday, write a book, work at a job. It's the awareness of interpretation, of judgment, decision, weighing, pondering.

The problem is that the first attention, as we grow older, becomes so strong that it blocks out the second attention.

That doesn't really have to be. But it occurs in our world because the people of our world are scared to death ... of life.

And they're even more scared of death—death not simply meaning the cessation of physical life, but anything that lies beyond the boundary of what we would call the normal.

But what's normal? I mean, what is sane, anyway? Sanity is just an agreement.

You and I are on an island together. And we're going to sit down and we're going to have a discussion and we're going to come to terms, and we're going to decide what is rational and what is irrational, what is sane and what is insane.

So for us, if someone spends hours gazing at the coconut tree that's on the island and worshiping it, we would say they're absolutely mishuganeh—they're crazy. Someone else on another island, two other people, see that the coconut tree is God and they worship it. And anyone who doesn't worship that tree is obviously crazy.

Sanity. Insanity. Well, I suppose we could say that sanity is the ability to function within a social structure or social group, and insanity is the inability to perceive and follow the rules of a particular group, to not agree with them or to be unaware of them.

Insanity simply really means that a person sees in other planes of consciousness.

There are no hallucinations.

There are only different forms of reality.

Some appear to be pleasant, some unpleasant, depending upon our values of interpretation. What does all this add up to? Well, if you get out your calculator for a second, we'll figure it out. That's the first attention. The first attention wants to add it up, divide it, multiply it.

I'm sitting up here now, looking in the direction of the volcano and the power is shifting. The luminous lines of energy that surround the Hawaiian Islands are moving and shifting now. I'm in the second attention.

From the point of view of the first attention, I couldn't see this. I would just see land, water, sky.

But in the second attention I blend with that awareness. I move freely into the astral worlds.

In the first attention, Hawaii is a series of islands—little dots out in the middle of the South Pacific, categorically owned by the United States, a place where people live, vacation. It has a history. Another race once inhabited it, and now they've been mostly reduced to selling beads and trinkets, like the American Indians on the mainland.

I won't see too much of Hawaii if I look with my first attention, will I? Resorts, a few houses, beaches, five or six islands.

Ah, but when I'm in the second attention, when I stop looking through eyes that have been formed for me by others, I see something else. I see power. I see one of the clearest spots on earth.

These islands are located around a series of inter-dimensional vortexes. Places of power. Places where it's very easy to step from one world into another.

And just sitting here talking to you, I walk from one world into another. Within milliseconds I shift through thousands of planes of reality. Seeing and experiencing them? No, not really. Being each one. For a moment, I am that awareness. Then I am another awareness and then another awareness. It's easier to do that here.

That's why it's good to visit Hawaii if you're seeking power. You don't really need to live here. Just to come over for a week is enough. Switzerland is another spot like this. It's very similar. These are the two clearest spots—Switzerland and Hawaii. Each opens up into different worlds, different planes of existence.

The lines of luminosity here, if you could see them in the subtle physical, stretch from island to island.

Yet each island's lines are a different color, and they're kind of unique. The energy moves in a circular form, usually counterclockwise around the islands, and then there are vortexes of energy above and below the islands.

And as you're here on your stay, if you meditate without trying too hard, you'll find it's very easy to be pulled up into these vortexes.

And you'll spin, you'll dance in them.

It's a dreaming vortex. A dreaming vortex is a place where it's easy to change. Because as we all know life is just a dream, yes?

But sometimes we get in a dream and it goes on, and on, and on, and it's not always a really exciting dream. So you've come to a dreaming vortex to step from one dream into another, from one world into another—to change, in other words.

If you've been living on the mainland or in Europe or Asia or wherever, and you've been leading a tight life—you've been meditating; gradually refining your life, tightening it up; eliminating the places, the people, the events that cause you to lose power; becoming more humble, friendlier; developing a sense of humor; learning to still the mind—then when you come to a place like this, you have built up a great deal of personal power, of energy.

Your kundalini is at a high point.

Then if you come here and you just let go—particularly, of course, in the late afternoon or in the evening, or the very early morning—then you'll find it's very easy to change.

You won't go back to the mainland or Europe or Asia. Someone else will. Your old self will have just washed away. Effortlessly.

Well, I don't know if it was effortless, in that all the time you spent preparing, the way you shaped your life, made it possible. But then when you come to a place of power like this, it appears to be effortless. And in fact, it is.

There are spirits here, forces. They're very protective and very good and they watch over these islands.

And I must confess, they're not entirely happy with what they see here, with the way the civilization is moving. But they're patient. They've been here for a long time, and they'll be here long after human beings have ceased to inhabit the islands.

What can we learn from these forces, from these spirits? What can we learn from Hawaii? Hawaii is not a place; it's a state of attention.

Oh, if you're down in Waikiki, on the beach, where the bikinis are hot and the sun is hotter, perhaps you won't learn too much about power that you couldn't learn any place else in any other beach.

But if you find a solitary beach, or you come up on top of a mountain, on top of the volcanoes and you sit for a while and you just still your mind, then awareness is all.

Then you can easily move from the first attention into the second attention. Then your being expands beyond the horizon of this world.

There're so many worlds beyond this world.

And as I've said before, we have the first attention—which is the awareness, the functional awareness of the world, which should guide us through life but often asserts itself to such an extent that it cuts us off from what we truly are, from most of our being and our perceptions. The second attention, of course, is that fluid awareness that we slide in and out of, in which we feel and come to know the other dimensional planes. Beyond that is the totality. Enlightenment. We call it enlightenment; it's a strange word for it. To enter the totality, to return into it, is beyond enlightenment.

So anyway, here I am in Hawaii. Cars are zipping by. There's a golden streak of light as the sun is getting lower on the horizon now, moving across the water.

And I think of you, sitting there, feeling the power of the island. This is the newest of the islands. It's still being formed. This is where the volcanoes still erupt.

You're still being formed. You're one of the newer islands. You're still erupting. These eruptions are cataclysmic—smoke, fire, flame. Something spews forth—hot lava. And then it hardens and forms. First it's just black and dark. Then, over a period of time, it softens. Things begin to grow there. Eventually it turns to white sand or soft earth.

The kundalini is a volcano. The kundalini energy shoots up your spine, and it's an eruption in your life.

Everything changes. Everything seems to be cataclysmic. Things are in proportion, out of proportion. Your relationships change. Your understandings of life and the world change. Everything shifts.

It's not something that you should try to control. It's not something that you can control any more than we can control the volcanoes here.

We can simply watch with awe and admiration. It's the process of life that's working within us.

And work within us it does.

You're looking for awareness. You're looking for power. And a good search it is. Where will you find it?

You'll find it first and foremost in your heart—in love. Love is the strongest power in the universe. Love is unity.

There are two forces at work, at play in the universe—unity and diversity. Unity is enlightenment. Diversity is illusion or maya, ignorance.

The more unity a person sees, not simply abstractly conceptualizes, but the more unity that they actually perceive, [then] the more spiritually advanced they are. The less unity they perceive, of course, the more diversity, the less evolved their attention is.

You've been a seeker for many lives. You've meditated, but now you're in a world of diversity. You see things through a glass darkly. There's separation everywhere. You're separate from your body. You're separate from your emotions. You're separate from the people around you. You're separate from the things that you would like to be or have or achieve.

That's because you're in the first attention. You're in the bardo of separativity.

Above that is the second attention, which is a plane of attention where we really don't see that things are separate.

We see that everything is connected by luminous strands of light—that life is a matrix of energy, that everything is one, and beyond that, of course, is the totality, where even concepts like unity are a dime a dozen. [Rama laughs.]

So then, your journey is to unity. And you need to think more about unity and focus on it. Now, what is unity?

Unity means strength through oneness. United we stand, divided we're in big trouble.

There aren't that many evolved people on the Earth. They've got to stick together. If we don't stick together, if we don't make a ring of power, then it's very easy for the forces of diversity to attack us, to keep us down.

When we're united, no force can interfere with us—because that is the strength of enlightenment. Enlightenment exists in every plane, in every world, any car, any color! Enlightenment is all.

So we could say that, when you step out of enlightenment—you could say "out of grace," if you're religious—we step into the world of diversity. We see things as separate.

That's what the Garden of Eden myth is all about—aside from a preoccupation with snakes that Adam had—he had trouble with snakes. Eve seemed to get along with them pretty well. Make of it what you will.

But there was unity in the garden. Everything was one, in other words. There was harmony.

The garden is the representation of the fruition—no death. You see, there's no death in enlightenment. But diversity—when our consciousness descended, suddenly the garden wasn't a garden. It wasn't paradise.

Hawaii is supposed to be paradise. It's only paradise if you see its unity. It's easier to see the unity here. That's why people call it paradise, not simply because it's warmer.

They don't realize that they're moving through these vortexes of energy here. And it's easier to see unity here than it is in New York City or in Chicago, L.A., Boston, Detroit, London, Paris, Tokyo, Bombay.

It's easier to see unity here. The doorway is open. But that doesn't mean that if you live here you will become enlightened more quickly. Not at all. Actually, it might be slower.

This is a place to come to remember—to remember what unity is.

You see, there's a terrible tendency in spiritual people, people who meditate, to all want to do their own thing. No one likes groups. Everybody wants to be independent. Everybody wants to assert themselves. No one likes to listen anymore.

Of course, if we just look at nature, we'll see what happens. We've got a big herd of gazelles. A couple of hunting lions, what do they hunt? The one that strays from the pack. It's an easy one for them to get. That's why human beings gather together in nations and city-states.

Why do we have trouble in the world? Because people don't understand unity.

If they understood unity, if they saw that we were all brothers and sisters, that we were all one, there would be no wars, there'd be no violence. There'd be no poor; we'd all be rich [Rama laughs.]

But people are in the *bardo.* Do you see what I'm saying?

In other words, you will see life and existence according to the plane of attention that you're in.

> And if you're in the plane of attention of diversity, then no matter where you are, that's what you'll see.

> If you're in the plane of attention of unity, then no matter where you are, that's what you'll see.

The first attention is diversity; the second attention is unity.

And beyond the second attention, of course, is the totality, which is beyond description but that which is most wonderful, most perfect.

Someday you may greet the totality in this lifetime. And if you do, even if you merge with that totality for a short time, then you'll understand.

So it's necessary for us to band together.

We've seen so much of diversity. In religions we see it. One religion proclaims itself to be the best, and all the others are supposed to be inferior. So religion obviously doesn't create unity, even just the hierarchies within a singular religion.

So that means that people in religion are still in the first attention.

That's why we practice what we call mysticism or higher spirituality. Where unity is the theme, rules and regulations really don't matter. We have a strong first attention because it's good to function in the world.

But what matters is unity. Unity is the universe. Unity is the world.

How do you go about perceiving unity? I mean, it could just sound like another word to you.

Well, when you stop thought, that's unity. Thought is diversity.

After you've been meditating for some time, you'll find that you'll think less, just during the day. You'll be in more of a unified attention—unified in the sense that you will see and be able to flow freely through the second attention, through all those multiple planes.

Nothing will interfere with that. It's not something you necessarily seek, it just happens because there's no obstruction.

That's unity.

Unity is the recognition of your tremendous power. If you could see how powerful you are, what you are like in other planes of awareness, then you'd realize there's nothing that can stop you.

Who am I? I'm enlightenment.

I come from a place far, far from here. Far not so much in a geographical sense—it's a sense of awareness. I come from the plane of unity and the plane of enlightenment.

And I've come into this world, into the world of diversity, to talk about unity. And I enjoy diversity. It's fun. The world is fun.

But unity is eternal. Diversity is transitory. Diversity is the world of death. There's no death in unity. There's no death in enlightenment. There's no suffering. There's only perfection.

So it's important to lead a unified life if you're seeking power. Power is in unity.

And that's why in the *I Ching,* the book that is about unity and diversity, we're told to join an organic fellowship of beings, to unify ourselves with others, if you're not capable of starting one.

In other words, if you're not enlightened, if your attention fields don't exist in all places at all times—of which there are naturally very few people on earth who are in that condition—then what you should do is join together with others who seek unity. That's what they mean by an organic fellowship.

And you should be with each other, spend physical time with each other. Because that is a symbol of unity, just the fact that you're spending time together, as opposed to everybody being off doing their own thing. Even on a physical level, that's unity.

It's fun to be alone. It's fun to spend time by yourself because then you can experience a different type of unity—your unity with the cosmos, your unity with all of life—and in silence when you're out walking in the woods or reading a book or meditating, strolling by the ocean or off on a mountain, whatever it is.

When there's no one else around, no one else's thought forms, the mind becomes quiet. No one to distract you. It's very easy to feel the unity of life, that pulse flowing, and that's a good thing to do.

But that's only one type or experience of unity.

The other unity we experience is communal. It's shared experience.

In other words, don't think of us as separate beings.

Imagine that we were once one body and it's been split into millions.

And when we get together, even on a physical level, even on the gross physical level, that suggests unity.

When we sit in the meditation hall together and meditate, when we take a trip together, when we go out to dinner together, whenever you get together with someone else who is drawn to unity, who seeks that eternal perfection, then that is unity itself in action, reflecting all the way down through the physical.

Unity, oneness, is a principle. It is enlightenment. Any movement in that direction is a movement towards enlightenment, and that's why the heart is always recommended—and love.

Because love is the principle of unity. It's the principle that unites. Love seeks to bring things together—the hexagram of "holding together." Love unites and joins things.

And so, if you seek unity, if you meditate on the heart, if you meditate on love in other words, you'll find that suddenly you'll enter into a different attention field, an attention field in which you see oneness, in which you see unity in even the most simple things—household products, your friends, people who don't love you, people who hate you.

You can see through the eyes of love. Unity. Love is a step on the way to enlightenment.

The greatest power in the universe is the power of unity, of oneness. All other powers are secondary because it is the only power that outlasts death. Death is the power of separativity; it separates us. But enlightenment is not affected by life or death. It is unity itself, incarnate and disincarnate.

Meditation is a celebration. When we meditate, we're celebrating unity. We're celebrating oneness.

And we're unifying our attention field. When you sit down to meditate and you practice your exercises—gazing, concentration—and you move into meditation, just what are you doing?

Well, ultimately, you're unifying yourself with the cosmos. That is to say, you're dropping the first attention that sees everything in division.

It's like a pair of sunglasses that colors everything. You're taking them off and seeing life more clearly.

You're seeing the unity in all of life and all of existence—the perfect oneness. It's flowing through you.

And the more unified your consciousness is, meaning the less separativity, the more you drop the first attention, [then] the more enlightened you are, the more aware you are.

I'm in Hawaii at 3,000 feet, yet I'm with you. Unity.

And what flows through my heart flows through the hearts of all beings who love—[in] this world and all worlds.

But more than our love of the separate, the worlds in which we see the unity, is our love of the totality—the oneness—which is not a concept but an actual experience.

So when you could be angry with someone and separate yourself from them, don't do that.

If you have people who are difficult to deal with, be neither attracted nor repulsed.

Go a step higher. Don't even think about it, and just feel the unity of the cosmos. The cosmos is perfectly united, and the higher the plane of attention, the more you'll perceive unity.

And one day, of course, as I've said before, you'll go beyond high. You'll go even beyond what I could call unity and you'll greet the totality of your being—your everything-ness, your nothingness.

Practice love in little ways. In other words, feel it, live it, let it flow through you. Give yourself a break. Give everybody else a break.

It doesn't matter. All hell can be breaking loose all around you and inside you. Just be still inside yourself and love.

You don't even have to love anyone in particular. Just love. Just feel that.

Sit down and meditate in the evening, when you do your evening meditation, and meditate on love. Just let it flow through you until you start to smile.

And your smile grows larger and larger until it's so big that you don't even feel it anymore—you don't feel the body—till all the thoughts stop and there's nothing but unity, there's nothing but oneness.

Feel your unity in nature. Take walks in nature. It's so easy to feel there because the green world is unified.

Feel your unity with members of your own sex. It's so easy to do.

Women need to feel that more. Men feel that, but women need to feel that more. They're so competitive with each other because of the way men have structured the world. Men have turned one woman against another because they set up a situation where women have to compete for men, and so sister can't trust sister.

Forget all that nonsense. Unite with other women.

There's strength in unity.

Think of the Earth as your body, the sky as your mind, the totality as your soul. Walk in that all day and all night long. Live in that perfect unity of being. Experience it. That's truth, freedom and perfection.

There's really nothing else worth living for, is there?

Everything else, the moments in diversity or moments of unhappiness and frustration—unhappy not even because we experience or don't experience anything in particular, but simply because we know we're not in that unified condition, which is what we really are and who we really are.

My name is Rama. And I love you. Not just on an individual basis but the totality which you represent, and which I serve, which I owe my allegiance to, and which all things are part of.

Join together with those you love, and love more, and add more to the circle. Let the circle grow larger and larger. Unify yourself with beings of like mind.

Don't be concerned with those who are in diversity.

That's the experience of the cosmos that the cosmos is having, in and through itself.

Let it happen. Don't be concerned.

You can see the unity in that if you're in a high level of attention.

The sun is just about to reach the water now. The clouds are very thick, and there's a stillness here. I look down and there are no houses, just rolling lava fields, some covered with grass that are older and have worn down a little bit, some in the distance that are black, closer to the shore.

I'm on the Kona Coast and yet I'm with you, and I'm in your heart, and I'm in all places at all times.

I'm always easy to find. Enlightenment is easy to find.

Look within yourself. Look within the things that make you high. Look towards unity, and you'll always find me there.

I am unity. The oneness of all life. Beyond life and death. Beckoning to you!

So meditate on the oneness. Become it.

And lighten up a little bit and give us all a break. Self-importance, ego, separativity—that's a yuck!

It's more fun to be in the circle of power. And when you make a circle of power with those you love, then that circle of power will protect you.

But if you find fault with each other and criticize each other instead of helping each other, well then, now you've gone to the consciousness of diversity, and now you're easy. The lions can pick you off—the lions of diversity.

But if you join together, then you are that principle of unity, you are the principle of enlightenment.

So join together with those who seek eternity, and see the unity in them. Watch the principles of unity acting through them.

Serve them, help them, but look beyond them too, to that which they really are, which is not a human being but the cosmos expressing itself.

Unity. Never leave the body without it.

CHAPTER THREE

MAGIC

Today is April the 25th, and it's around twenty-five of six in the early evening. I'm at around 6,000 feet at Lake Tahoe, and today I'm going to talk to you about magic.

I'm parked here facing the lake on a small beach, and there's some early evening commuter rush hour traffic behind me. Not too much, since this is an interesting time of year here, in-between the ski season and the beach season so it's not very crowded—it's a good time to come here.

In the distance I see the snow-covered mountain peaks, and on the other side of the lake the waves are rolling in. Tahoe is more like an ocean, I think, than a lake—an ocean that's 6,000 feet above sea level.

Magic. What's magic? Life is magic. Death is magic. Time is magic, space.

Magic is the ability to perceive beyond the surface. We say that something is magical because it's not logical. It doesn't fit into the ordered scheme of things, which is what makes it worthwhile, because we all know that everything that fits in the ordered scheme of things can drive us completely up the wall after a while. So magic really has nothing to do with that at all.

Magic is our awareness of the timelessness of time—real magic, that is. Oh, there is the magician who struts and frets his hour upon the stage, pulls rabbits out of hats, hats out of chipmunks [Rama laughs], does all kinds of great things through the sleight of hand, the quick blurred movement, through distraction.

But there's another kind of magic, which is really a science. It is the ability to move awareness and to do literally anything with it.

What can you do with awareness? You can change yourself, you can change someone else, you can change the universe, anything.

But in order to really practice magic, you need to study in the school of awareness for a while.

The school of awareness is the school of mysticism.

Mysticism is the experience of eternity, of that which lies beyond the physical phenomenal experience. Not that that is even what it appears to be.

Taking a walk isn't really taking a walk, taking a shower isn't taking a shower, living isn't living, dying isn't dying. It only appears to be that way because of the centering of our awareness.

So the school of awareness is really perception. Everything is perception. And perception, as you know, is limited by the way that you think. When I say "think," I don't simply mean word thoughts—ideas that come through your mind in terms of language—I am speaking, and you're hearing my voice.

But there's also a language that takes place not only in the conscious mind but in the subconscious. It is a language of categorization—always trying to fit your experiences into a little box, to make everything work out, to make everything seem uniform.

Now, magic is not categorical. It is not really uniform. That's what makes it interesting. It is beyond ... logic. It is beyond time and space.

And in order to practice magic, of course, you need only one thing—awareness, what we might call power.

Now, everybody has a certain degree of awareness. Everyone is awareness. But people are aware of so little.

Within you there are thousands of rings of luminosity, bands, and each one is a universe of perception. In the average person's lifetime, they might just open up two or three, maybe only four of those bands.

Those bands are keys to doorways that lead to other universes, other understandings of life, other experiences, other selves; we have other selves.

You see, that's the magic, isn't it now?

We have other selves that are not of this world, of this time, of this cycle.

We are ancient beings, evolving forward and backwards simultaneously. We are not structured in time. That only appears to be to the uneducated eye, or the over-educated eye.

We are eternal travelers, eternal voyagers—appearing to be here when in fact we are somewhere else.

Magic has a lot to do with parallel realities.

Parallel realities are everywhere. They are not necessarily parallel, sometimes they're tandem. Sometimes they're not in any uniform, geometrical progression. Something beyond that progression, that is the totality.

The totality is our existence. All magic comes from the totality. And your ability to peruse the halls of magic, let alone to participate in it, to use it, is really very much dependent upon your ability to experience or open yourself up to different aspects of the totality.

In this world, there are only aspects. Beyond this world then, there is something else.

Beyond all worlds and all conditions, we have the totality—nameless, formless, colorless, odorless, tasteless—complete being, beyond conception.

That's why I use the word "totality," not something finite. For me a totality is not finite. It is not a sum total. It is not the end product of the addition of a column of mathematical figures.

If we put five people together, are there really five people? I don't think so, not in the world of magic.

In the world of magic, there is only one being, reflecting itself in countless forms, playing hide and seek with itself throughout the universes.

Why are those universes there? Why is there life? Why is there death? Search me! Maybe you'll find an answer.

Magic doesn't really give us answers. It gives us questions— questions about identity, about the movement of time and space, about the elementals—earth, water, fire, ether.

How are things constructed? How are they put together?

There is a form for everything, kind of a template that exists, not in this world, but in another universe, another world.

When you understand that form, when you've seen it, perhaps in dreaming, perhaps in kind of a supra-wakefulness, then you can use that form. You can create through that form, you can become it.

Everything that you see here, in other words, is a reflection of a higher reality.

This particular world is not really a world, it's a perception that you're having at the moment. The alteration of your perception will create an alteration of the world. That's magic.

You can actually alter the world through perception. I'm not saying this just in a subjective sense. Let me give you an example.

If your awareness was strong enough, you can change the fate of a whole world ... without ever leaving your room.

The interactions you have with human beings, from now on until the day you die, all of those interactions are controlled by something.

You will meet one person and not another. You'll shop in one store and have an experience there, and not another. You will feel love towards one person and fear towards another and indifference towards another.

What's happening? Why is this all taking place?

There is an order—not order in the express sense of a uniformed army marching in perfect cadence, boots-polished order; balanced equations. No.

Celestial order is a perfect disarray. The idea of order, the very concept, is something that we've forced upon the universe. There is no such thing.

There is no such thing as mind or matter or spirit.

What exists is existence—undefinable, unapproachable, yet something that you can experience. That's how you gain power—by experiencing life.

Different powers are gained by different experiences.

So the clever perceiver determines the power they wish to have and molds their experiences accordingly.

If you're powerful enough you can even determine whom you will meet and whom you will avoid long before.

What will happen in those encounters? Who knows? It wouldn't be much fun if you knew all of that—you'd just be watching an old video called your life.

Everything happens in dreams. Not the dreams that you have at night.

There is another type of dreaming. That's the magic. There is another world where things are, if I can use the phrase—I'll give myself permission, I can — more real than they are here.

More real. What does that mean?

It means flooded awareness—awareness so full that there's no sense of the particular, where time doesn't mean anything, where there is no space, individualized being.

There is a flux of existence someplace where everything is prefigured. All these forms, these apparently random forms we see, exist there.

The Earth is the fun house, the big giant mirrors that distort things. You stand in front of one mirror and you look bigger. You stand in front of another one, you look fat; another one, you look skinny; another one, you look like a shrimp.

That is what this world is—it's a world of mirrors. It is only a world of reflections.

None of this exists.

All important decisions in the universe occur someplace else.

That is the place that you go to in your dreams. That is where your dreams come from, another world.

I'm here at Lake Tahoe. It's the early evening, but the sunlight is still quite bright. There are shadows across the beach, and the sun is glistening off the snow on top of the peaks in the distance, the Sierras. I'm on the northern side of the lake in Nevada, and there's magic at 6,000 feet.

You exist someplace else, and when you can contact yourself in that other place, when you can open up a kind of an inter-dimensional phone line between yourself and your various selves, when you become aware of that, that's when magic begins.

The self that you have here is a kind of a cardboard self that has been colored in. It is only partial. But as you contact your other selves, then you become more real.

There is another world—a world of dreams.

It's funny because we say that a dream is not real.

If I was to stop somebody, if I was to go stand in front of one of these cars, stop the car, and have the guy roll down the window and look at him with kind of a crazed look in my eye, like I'd just come down from the mountains where I'd been for too long, [Rama laughs] and I grab the guy, and I say, "Listen! I gotta know—I need to know, what's real?" [Rama affects a crazed voice]

Meanwhile, the poor guy's freaking out! But he figures, "Maybe,

maybe if I just pacify him, I'll just be able to get out of here. What does he want?"

And I've got this gleam in my eye, and I say, "Now look, what—is this real around me, or are the dreams real? Is it real?" And he says, "Oh, of course it's not real—a dream is not real. This is real. See, look around you. This is real. Dreams aren't real!" And then I'd say, "Oh." And then I'd disappear. And he'd be left wondering if it ever happened.

Well, it just happened, didn't it, in the world of dreams.

Dreams are real. This is unreal. This world is unreal. Everybody has it backwards. This is the dream. This is an insubstantial pageant. Nothing here lasts. That is how you know it's the dream.

You're confused, I can see. You're confused. You have thought all your life that all this is —that this is a real world. And that when you sleep, and you dream, which is just one type of dreaming, you believe that's not—I see, I understand. Oh, no wonder you're confused. Gosh!

You see, what I've done is come into your dream. Your life is a dream, is what I'm saying. You just don't realize it. You are asleep.

You are really someplace else, your body. And I've just stepped into your dream for a while.

Now, the funny thing is, there are all these other characters in your dream. The people you see in your life and you've known, they're all in your dream. I realize that. And they don't realize it's a dream either.

I'm the only one, or one of a few anyway—the only one who's talking to you at the moment. I know because I'm awake in the dream.

That's the art of dreaming, you see, to be awake in the dream. But anyway, that's the magic. If you're awake in the dream and you know it's a dream, you can do anything.

Let me explain it to you in another way.

Let's say that you—after you listened to this—you put your head down on the pillow and you fall asleep. In your sleep, you're in a dream. You are in some strange place. Maybe you're here at Lake Tahoe, maybe you're in Egypt, maybe you're in a laundromat, who knows? You are someplace.

And suddenly you're in a dream, and it's the usual mish-mash. Suddenly you say to yourself, "By gosh, I'm in a dream." You wake up and you say, "I know I'm asleep, and that this is a dream."

Well, when you realize that, then you can do anything, can't you? Because you can make anything happen in a dream. In a dream you can fly; you can go meet anybody that you want to.

You can create a civilization, a universe, anything you want to do because, of course, the material of the dream, the fabric of the dream world, is pliant. Imagination there, is reality, yes?

But of course if you don't know that, then you're just sort of subjected to whatever happens in the dream—not necessarily much fun.

So then, what I'm postulating is that this is a dream. This is the dream we're in now. But you don't realize that.

People wonder sometimes, well, why Rama, can you do certain things with energy and light and appearances? Why can you do those things and we can't do them? Why can you take us out into the desert and make the mountains dissolve and shimmer and, you know, do all the little Rama-esque things that I do?

Why can you do—why can you change our awareness field?—all the so-called miracles, which are not miracles from my point of view.

My answer is obviously that I realize that this is a ridiculous dream I'm in, and since I realize it, I can probably do just about anything I'm in the mood to do.

Because it's just a dream. The only reason I can do it and you can't do it, is because I know I'm awake in this dream and I can do these things, but you don't believe that you can because you're bound by the dream.

Something like that. It's a way of trying to explain something that's basically inexplicable, of course.

That's magic, you see. The magic is the realization of the dream.

Now, of course there is another plane that you're not aware of at the moment—at least the part of you that I'm addressing is not aware of—and that is that which is real.

The reality.

And the reality isn't in just one place or one experience or one time zone. It is not just one dimension.

But it's a place where everything is real. Not that it's a place—it could be a place.

Everything there is real. There is nothing but reality.

And that's where the dream comes from. The dream is the reflection in an interestingly chaotic, yet perfectly harmonious, way of that.

Now, I can tell you're interested in magic. If you want to know, "Well, how do I do it, how do I, how—?" Well, I'm telling you how, exactly.

Right now you're standing on one shore. OK, here I am on Lake Tahoe. I'm looking out and I can see the water. Across the water there are these mountains, and there's another shore. I'm here.

If a fog rolled in right now, I would not be able to see the mountains, and if this was my first experience here at Lake Tahoe, I would not know there were mountains over there, even though there are these huge 12,000 foot mountains over there.

I would be unaware of that. And then when the fog rolls back, I can see the mountains. Voila! They are there!

To practice magic you have to first get a sense that there's something on the other side—that there is another side. So the first condition is learning how to see.

To see is to experience beyond the self-created shadows of doubt that you are immersed in—to look through time. To be clairvoyant, in other words. To see the other shore.

Now, with that seeing, a kind of magic has begun.

And that seeing occurs, of course, through stopping thought. Thought is the fog. When thought stops in meditation, at any point, when there's no thought, we see the other shore.

Now, the funniest thing—I'll tell you the funniest thing—when you see the other shore, if you were to take out a pair of binoculars—it would be very hard to see otherwise—if you'd look, you would see someone waving at you frantically, with a huge grin, on the other shore.

And it would be you. You are waving back at yourself. Finally you managed to get her to wake up a little bit, and you're waving back at yourself. You managed to penetrate the dream mists, and she's awake and she's looking back at you.

I'm referring, of course, to the you on the other shore. This is the one who's aware, who's smiling. The one who is just becoming aware, who is looking through the binoculars and doesn't really believe what she sees—that, I suppose, is the one you call yourself.

When thought stops, the world stops, life stops, death stops, time stops, space stops, and thoughts.

That's the magic—stopping thought.

Well, I don't know if it's—nothing can happen. The dream is so thick. The maya is so thick. There's no magic as long as there's all this thought.

So the first condition for the practice of higher magic is the stopping of thought. And the stopping of thought, of course, comes about through practice, through love, self-giving, by learning how to increase awareness—the study, of course, of self-discovery.

Now, stopping thought is only the beginning.

As Brahmananda, who was a disciple of Sri Ramakrishna, once remarked, "The inner life begins with samadhi." This is an awesome thought, I realize, for the average person who meditates, that it can begin with samadhi. Because most people consider when they've reached samadhi that that's the end.

Samadhi is the absorption in the Self, the self in the Self.

There are different types of samadhi—Salvikalpa samadhi, Nirvikalpa—different designations of fields of attention far beyond this world.

The average individual spends many, many lifetimes meditating and seeking and chewing bubblegum and doing things like that to attain the experience of samadhi. And so people feel, "Phew! Oh! I've made it to samadhi! Boy, this is it! Graduation day!"

Well, then you have to go out and get a job. Or go to graduate school.

So stopping thought is really wonderful [Rama laughs], ecstatic, perfect.

There is nothing to worry about. You spend much too much time worrying. There's nothing to lose and there's nothing to gain in a dream—because the dream changes so quickly. Why bother to get stuck in it?

There are just endless reflections in the mirror. Various forms—everything you see around you is yourself. Everyone you see is an extension of yourself—every caterpillar, every butterfly, every metamorphosis is yourself.

You are changing infinitely, and that part of you which is aware of all of this, which gives it life and form, will only be for a while. Metamorphosis, change—something old, something new, something timeless.

So the magic begins just beyond the realm of thought, in that perpetual silence of the void, where all the forms that have ever been or will ever be are there, kind of in a huge bank, a flux.

They float there—everything, all eternities, all possibilities—just float there, in a perfect sea of awareness.

So the art of magic, then, is the transformation of the self. It's the ability to go into that flux, the totality. To enter into it consciously, and when you've entered into it consciously, you reorder.

You see, we're like an atomic structure.

We've got a causal body that's linked together. The energy strands and bands of our being are linked in a certain way—makes us what we are. It causes us to perceive a certain level of the dream of life.

But you can reorder those. That's magic, you see.

The being you are now can't practice a lot of magic, or a lot of the magic that you practice is kind of black magic, a rough magic, an unhappy magic.

But when you throw yourself into the totality, you reorder yourself. This happens when you die.

When you die, your being dissolves and it reorders. It goes back into the totality. And then it comes back again as something new, another form, a more evolved form.

But it's not necessary to die to do this. You just have to enter into the flux again. That's the magic because then you will become being and becoming, metamorphosis—the caterpillar or butterfly—is it the same? Is the butterfly an extension of…? No, it's not.

The butterfly has nothing to do with that caterpillar. Metamorphosis, change in the cocoon—one thing becomes another.

Two dreams come together in a dreaming vortex.

There is a transition from one dream to another.

That's the interesting point, of course, for the advanced student of existence. Not one form or the other, neither the caterpillar nor the butterfly, but the moment of transformation.

Because at that moment, oh nobly born one, the clear light of reality presents itself—it is possible to slip between the worlds.

The art, I will admit, for the beginner and the intermediate magician, is simply to be able to transform, to change the self at will into something other. And when you understand the body of perception, when you've stored enough energy and light and power, you can transform yourself into anything.

The consummate magician is not interested in simply becoming something else, having done that—that's just changing horses in midstream—but rather to slip through between dreams and to become everything, to merge with the totality.

That's the consummate art of self-discovery.

Between the dreamer and the dream, there is something. There is no way to describe it. I could refer to it as an opening, but an opening into what?

Lao Tzu says, "From wonder into wonder, existence opens."

So magic, then. There are different types of magic, aren't there? It all has to do with perception—the miracle of perception, the miracle of awareness. How aware are you? How aware would you like to be? Would you like to wake in this dream? Would you like to change into other things? To possess powers, to change, to be everything, to be nothing?

There are beings on the other side who will help you. There are beings in between who will attempt to thwart you. There are beings who are completely indifferent. Powerful beings.

Because there are various levels of dream, there are various levels of creation. And some levels of creation are very aware of other levels, and some are oblivious.

Most of the people on our Earth are totally oblivious to the other levels of creation, to the different dimensional planes and the beings that inhabit them.

But you should know that this world is but a fish bowl for some, and you are a fish swimming.

There are beings that look into this world and other worlds and see clearly. Some of those beings are what you would call good, and some are what you would call harmful, negative, evil, and some are indifferent.

They exist in planes of light and fields of perfect attention, and they are relatively unaware of the objective world as you know it, of this dream. They can penetrate it if they choose to, and doubtlessly, in their evolution they have experienced it. But now they just exist in fields of light and fields of perfection, perfect awareness, perfect attention.

How do you tell the good beings from the harmful ones? Well, usually by the kind of hat they wear. Seriously?

By how you feel when you encounter them.

When you encounter a higher being, you'll feel wonderful. Not just during but afterwards.

Always trust your feelings.

And as evidence of that, as I was speaking those lines, two beautiful geese just flew by in tandem. As you know, the goose is a sign, at least in the *I Ching*, it's a symbol of seeking, of the powerful seeker who flies into the infinite and attains different levels of attention.

Who's doing all this attaining, anyway? Who is the you who is having this experience? Who is dreaming all of this?

That is who you want to get to. Whom you wish to find.

The destructive beings will come to you in your sleep. Sometimes they'll come to you in the guise of another person. Sometimes they'll come to you in the guise of a sandwich. No? Well, it could happen. [Rama laughs.]

Why do they want to thwart you? Well, I don't know. It gets them through the day. Don't worry about it—just avoid them.

How do you avoid them? I would say, essentially, that inwardly we solicit what we experience.

If something in you wants what they represent, then they will come to you. They will feel a call.

If you only want light, if you only want love, if you only want to experience the limitless awareness of the totality or to practice the happy magic, then they don't come, really. Or if they do, they don't stay.

But if there's some part of you that wants to experience the darker side, then they come. Then they stay.

Even so, it is true that there are beings who come and interfere.

But when you realize who and what you are, they can't possibly interfere. They only interfere because you think that they're strong and that you're weak. When you realize that you are limitless and endless light, then how can they affect you?

How can the little fish swimming in the ocean affect the ocean? They aren't even noticed. So the trick then is to get into, of course, very high levels of attention, and then they just bounce right off.

How can you cultivate higher beings that exist on the other shore and get them to aid you? Well, the same way that you cultivate the interest of a teacher of self-discovery.

Not by the fact that you have a perfect smile but by the fact that your intent is pure, or that you've just stored a tremendous amount of energy. In other words, if you lead a tight life, if you evolve, then you have to draw the higher beings to you. It's the law of the universe.

So if you put your time into improving yourself instead of proving yourself, if you put your time and energy into meditation, into feeling eternity and to reaching for that other shore, then you're less and less concerned with the world.

Meaning not that you don't work or don't participate in society, but rather, just that your attention is elsewhere. If that's what matters, and if you practice the practices which I and others describe, or you just learn on your own, to increase your level of awareness—if you keep changing and growing, then they will come.

That's the promise of eternity to those who seek knowledge—a wonderful promise that's always fulfilled. Not simply will they come, but knowledge itself will come.

So magic, this rough magic, is the universe that is our lives. We exist unaware of what we are—until the magic comes.

The magic is awareness, and awareness frees us from the dream of life. It brings us to the reality. And there are so many different types of magic. There are so many levels of creation, of evolution.

But the important thing for you is to solidify your life, to play with it—to lose the ego, to become flexible and free, to learn to stop thought, to have compassion for all other beings—because all other beings are you.

To learn to trust life itself because that's all there is, is life. And to ignore these shadows, these self-important shadows in the dreamscape.

The people and places and events in this world are not real. This is a dream.

The dreamtime is the reality. That's elsewhere. That is the other shore. And you're dancing and singing and playing there already.

No matter what tragedy befalls you and no matter what hardship, don't be concerned with it. It is only a dream. You're already someplace else, thoroughly enjoying yourself in the cosmos.

And once you connect with that part of yourself, in the stillness, then you'll be free. Then you can assume any form of creation, no forms, or perhaps slip in between them to the totality.

The sun is almost set, and the shadows are consuming the mountains, as the shadow of our death some day will consume us.

Then a new day will come, and the mountains will be there again, but they won't be the same mountains—as we won't be the same. And yet at each moment, if you could be aware of it—there is life and death within us.

And we are being reborn and transformed at every second.

It's time to step outside of time—by willing it, by loving it, by reaching for it. You are the shadow of your own dreams, and your dreams are real. And I've come into your dream to remind you of that.

I, awake in the dream, to remind you to play and rejoice and to celebrate life, and to not fear death. Because all this is more wonderful than it seems. And life is real, and it is eternal. And dreams are real, and dreams come true. So have good dreams.

And if you don't, they'll pass. And if you do, they'll pass.

If you seek knowledge, the promise of knowledge is that you will reach the totality one day.

That will happen to you.

And the greatest wonder of wonders will befall you, to see and dance with your own perfect being—beyond form, beyond body, beyond attention, beyond all of this.

Reality.

So dream wonderful dreams. They'll come true.

So this is Rama, at 6,000 feet, on a lake that isn't a lake, in a Tahoe—that is the name of the model, curiously enough—four-wheel-drive Chevy mini-Blazer, that isn't really a truck, talking without a voice to people that don't exist.

CHAPTER FOUR

ELECTRONIC TRIBE

This is Rama. I'm talking to you from the twentieth century. I'm on the island of Nantucket. It's around 3:30 in the afternoon on the 29th of May, 1985. Nantucket is an island off the coast of Massachusetts, along the Eastern Seaboard of what they call North America.

I'm pulled off by the side of the road at a place of power. Cars are pulling back and forth, driving, stopping—a lot of tourists sight-seeing. I'm sitting here in the Porsche, thinking about the future, which occurred a long, long time ago, long before any of us can remember. It's windy out—the winds of time are blowing, the winds of change.

Chaos is everywhere, and chaos is wonderful. That's all there really is. There is no today. There is no tomorrow. There is only eternity, perfection, consciousness, power—and light.

Love unites the worlds; it's all that stands between us. Order is the creation of man.

Chaos is the natural condition. Chaos is perfection. There is only awareness. Don't be afraid of it. Learn to live on the edge and enjoy it because that's all there is.

There's only eternity, and you're it—part of everything that's ever been or will ever be, beyond abstraction, beyond conception.

It's ridiculous, if you ask me. I don't know what any of us are doing here. But we're a tribe, a network, cruising the galaxy. We have offices in every loka, in every part of existence. I suppose you make that out to be a unique situation. We're unique! No, I don't think so.

We're enlightenment. We are enlightenment. And we're bound together by perfection, realization and awareness.

Who are these human beings anyway, who walk around, strut, fret, as if they owned the planet, or the goddamned universe? I mean, who do they really think they are? Transitory beings, alive for a while, dead, then alive again, not even remembering their eternal glory—the passage through time and space that's so remarkable, that each of us makes.

I'm talking networks, awareness, infinite being—beyond conception. The house next door to yours, and maybe the way the plumbing works, the way the galaxy works, spinning each through each other, the dimensions, endless and perfect.

And we're a tribe, bound together by secrets, secrets that exist in other worlds. That's what makes us a tribe, our secrets.

We are the electronic tribe. Back again for another show before we hit the road and head out again to strange and perfect universes.

We're standing together here, even though I'm alone, and all beings that ever existed that are part of this network are in me. I comprise multitudes, even though some days I can hardly add or subtract, and you think it's all so great!

You're right, it's all great.

Perfect attention, there's nothing else. The electronic tribe.

I'd like to talk to you about where we've been, how we got into this mess. [Rama laughs.]

What's a network? A network is a group of beings who travel through time and space and dimensions together.

It's really one being. There is no separativity. There's only one being, but it divides itself into forms, countless forms.

And it spreads and winds its way throughout the universes—different beings existing in different planes simultaneously that are psychically connected by something so deep inside them that no one understands them.

At least not anyone who can be in time and space and in a body.

There are different networks that work the galaxies, the universes. I am part of a particular net: enlightenment. The network of enlightenment.

There are other nets; they're not connected. In this great chaos that is existence, this redolent, wonderful disorder that is life, each network cruises, endlessly moving, with no apparent motion, through all of the worlds.

A network is a tribe. And a tribe, as I mentioned before, is connected by its secrets.

A tribe is not a loose collaboration of beings who just get together in a powwow, who live together or work together. A nation is not a tribe. A family is not a tribe. A racial or ethnic group is not a tribe. Ancestry does not create a tribe, at least not bloodline.

What creates a tribe is a bond, a sharing of secrets. Not a secret that could ever be told in any words, but a secret that's much too wonderful for that—a secret that can only be told by the unfolding of one's life, specifically, your life.

This message is addressed to those of you who are part of the network, the tribe of awareness. Those of you who seek to find yourselves.

You lie in other dimensions. You live there.

This is only a small fraction of your being that's here in this body, in this time and space, on this planet.

There are different members of the tribe. The tribe is, of course, divided into male and female in this world. What is male and female? Is it just a physical condition, hormones?

No. The energy runs very, very differently in a woman than in a man.

What is a woman? A woman is chaos. Complete chaos.

Chaos is the naturally perfect state of all things.

A man, as we see a man in this age, in this world, is chaos, but he doesn't recognize that fact, so he tries to bring order into everything.

And order is disorder. Order creates disorder.

Chaos is not disorder. Chaos is the totality of existence.

You could call it God. You could use the term, the Tao. I like chaos. It means more to us in English. Chaos is all things—wild and wonderful, connected perfectly by the life force.

And a woman is more in touch with that chaos because of the way her being is.

Now there's something beyond the natural chaos that is woman or the chaos with implied order that is man, and that's the totality.

To stay as we are is not the issue, but to awake from the dream of life—to awaken and see what we really are, which is not this finite body, not the experiences that it has, not the memories from this life.

We are our most distant lifetimes. We are the experiences of other members of our network, and the question is, of course, what network are you part of?

I can only speak for the network I represent: the network of enlightenment. It's not a better network than other networks. It's just another network.

CBS, NBC, ABC—these are networks on television. Affiliated stations. They are all broadcasting, at some times, the same things. There are certain shows that are on. There are certain standards that are agreed on between all the stations.

They are linked. Yet each station is unique; each station has some independent programming. But they all have kind of a common carrier wave.

The network of enlightenment is the electronic tribe in this world. We live in an age that's repeating itself endlessly.

We're getting closer again to the techno-chic world we saw in Atlantis that occurs in countless planes. And it's indigenous to enlightenment.

This is a dark age. That's not news. It's a dark time, when we all have to be particularly aware of danger. Not danger in the sense that anyone can injure our spirits. Our spirits are eternal and perfect. But danger in the sense that other networks seek to interfere with the natural process of chaos. Enlightenment is chaos. Complete beyond conception.

So it's necessary to be aware of the difficulties of the time.

There are times, there are ages, when enlightenment is the natural way—when the path of love and selfless giving, and chaos, ecstasy, is the only guidepost, the only lighthouse in a dark and stormy sea. And all gravitate towards it naturally. But this is not an age like that, is it? Absolutely not.

This is a time of great confusion, of great darkness, when other networks are slipping in through other dimensional planes.

So soon this network will leave this Earth. But before we do, we have a few things to do. To accomplish? Not exactly. To be, perhaps is closer. There's no way to express it exactly.

I'm part of an ancient tribe of guardian beings who have a particular job in the universe.

We keep the dimensional planes open. We guard the secret power places that exist between dimensions. We represent the totality.

We exist everywhere in every universe; we've got at least a small office. We send our beings out, and they incarnate in a world, some physically, some not physically. They come in the subtle physical. They live in the etheric body.

We watch over a world and guide it, tenderly.

Not interfering in its natural course of evolution—is our way.

But there comes a time when a race of beings makes a decision, a choice as to what to do with its destiny.

And when they choose to reject enlightenment and accept something else, then again, there's no interference on our part. We leave peacefully.

It's the end of their world because the karma is inevitable. They have to destroy themselves.

The network of enlightenment is a very wide network. It's not relegated to a simple type of being. It's not the network of the goody-goodies, I'm afraid.

Countless forms make up this network.

But in this world, there are few of us now.

Most of the beings that are incarnating are on other nets, have other destinies. There's no way to describe it precisely because we're dealing with chaos, and to impose too much order on it will interfere with its own natural purity.

So then, here we are. I'm on the island of Nantucket. There are about 20 bicycles in front of me. Some kids just drove up and parked them, going over the path here down onto the beach. I'm parked by the side of the road, as is my way, stopping to chat with you for a while before I continue my drive.

The electronic tribe.

How do you exist in a world of darkness? A world where right is wrong, and wrong is right? Where it's difficult just to still your mind and meditate? Where threats of not only physical violence but inner corruption are everywhere?

You have to band together. There's a strength in unity. Unity is oneness, and oneness is the tribe.

It's easy to tell the evolutionary level of a group of beings, or an individual being, simply by examining their behavior, their art, their psychology, their thought forms, their lingual structures, their history, their present moment of course, their future ideas, the quality of their emotions.

You will always see, if this group is a highly evolved group or on the way up, a movement towards oneness. People joining together. The art will reflect it. The language will reflect it.

In this world, we see nothing but diversity. Language separates one country from another. People can't communicate. There isn't just one language, there are so many. Everybody lives in their own little fort, their little house, away and apart from all others. Everyone thinks separate ideas and wants to develop a separate identity.

They fight wars with each other. They destroy each other's identities. The strong conquer the weak. The weak serve the strong and hope to become strong so they can conquer others who are weaker than themselves.

This is the age of darkness.

The way for the tribe is to unite and to bring forward its knowledge from its other lives, which is the knowledge, of course, of sound, light, color, and energy.

Energy is our principle quality, the quality of our tribe.

This is the age of electrical energy. The age of atomic energy hasn't really dawned yet, not in the way that atomic energy has evolved in other worlds.

This is still a very primitive age, and I'm afraid they may not get much further here.

But those of us who are here, who incarnated in this world, join together. And we use the media, we use the electronic technology—which actually, to be honest with you, is largely ours—to consolidate us and give us strength. It's the computer era.

Well, who do you suppose invented computers? I mean, no one in particular, of course. But just speaking in terms that are relevant to you, in terms of Earth history, let alone other-worldly history, the computer, of course, came from Atlantis.

The computers in Atlantis were infinitely evolved as opposed to what we see today. The science, the technology, everything was really done with light. All processing was done with light, with crystal formations and structures. Electricity is much too slow.

Why do you suppose that in the last 50 years, 100 years, technology has evolved a thousand times further than it has in the last 2,000 or 3,000? Why this sudden awakening of the computer age when just a hundred years ago there weren't automobiles? And now, today, we have what we consider at least, complex computers.

Well, of course, it's the level of souls that are incarnating, that are coming in.

The old Atlantean souls, the members of the tribe, are coming back. And they have a natural affinity for communication, electronics, medicine, law and media. These are the qualities of the tribe.

It's necessary, if you're part of the tribe, to extend your awareness in these directions. In other words, you've done this before. There's a hidden strength in all of this for you.

You need something. Not just to get through the day, but to get through the incarnation. You need to find that power, that perfect unity. Meditation isn't simply stopping your thoughts and dissolving. It's that, but it's creating—creating and matching yourself against chaos and merging with it. It's finding the oneness.

The oneness is found in our work world in technology.

The old Atlantean sciences, in other words, from the tribe of enlightenment, of which there are only a few remnants and chards left in this world, were medicine, law, electronics—as you call it—computers, technology and performing, creating beauty, what you would call the performing arts—dance, music, networking energy, communication.

In the old civilization, law existed to create order, that is to say, to see that justice was done. When there is no law in the world of sentient beings, then everyone tries to impose their own law on everyone else, and that's the law of the strong. But in the old way, in the law of the tribe, the law was equal for all, equality for all. Not the strong win and the weak lose.

Medicine, of course, was evolved to heal—since healing is oneness.

Naturally, there's a thing we call death, old age, infirmity. Just as there are four seasons—the fall brings about decline, and the winter, I suppose, death, so that the spring and new life can come forth and come to fruition in the summer—so there's a spring and a summer and a fall and a winter of our lives, of our bodies.

Medicine doesn't seek to—Atlantean medicine, tribal medicine—to put an end to this at all. But what it does is weed the garden so things can grow clearly that need to grow, and things that have passed their prime can pass gently.

Computers are the center point, the center access—information processing based upon a spiral network, similar to that which is the chaos of existence itself, the analysis of systems, the interlocking lokas. In other words, computers are the study of existence itself in the sense that if it's truly done properly, it's one of the few arts, and it is indeed an art—at least the creation and writing of software is an art as opposed to a science—in which perfection is absolutely required.

Normally, as you know, a person can write a book or a piece of music. And in the writing of the music or the book, or in dancing, in any of the creative performing arts, or silent arts, or plastic arts, if a person makes a mistake, who's going to know? Well, they can just say it's part of the art even though our bodies feel there's something incorrect there. It's the same way in science. But in computers, it's fascinating because in the creation of software, everything has to be perfect because if it's not perfect, the program won't run. It's an art that demands a higher perfection. And when a person spends their time doing that, working on that, creating that, then what occurs is a different kind of magic.

In other words, what happens when you're sitting writing a program and you're bringing—you're joining together disparate parts.

What happens is something analogous happens inside yourself.

In other words, it's not a question of function. The purpose of writing a perfect program is not so much to create an end in itself, but the very process itself is the end. The end is not "the end." The means is the end.

Because at that moment when that creation occurs, enlightenment exists in a fragmented way; things join together.

And here come the kids, screaming, running for their bikes. They look like they're having a good time. Part of the redolent disorder of existence.

So where then, is truth in all of this? Where is it found? Well, to be blunt with you—if I can for a minute—truth is found everywhere. [Rama laughs.]

Truth is everywhere. And yet there's a particular truth that's applicable just for you. Well, what's the truth that's applicable just for you?

Survival. Survival doesn't simply mean keeping the body going. Survival means becoming complete. Not that there is a completion in a way.

So the tribe unites, it joins.

And as the tribe moves into a higher level of attention, there's less internal disagreement within the tribe. The tribe and the leader of the tribe are not separate, they're one. The members of the tribe get along. There's no jealousy. There's no fear. There's a common purpose that unites them.

In our world, in the world of the "Road Warrior" mentality, in our pre-World War III condition in which meditation is considered a cult activity, in which spiritual refinement is laughed at and in which people who practice self- discovery are actually persecuted and ridiculed, then it's necessary to be mobile.

A tribe is mobile; it doesn't stay in one place. It moves from one locale to another—from one, I suppose, hunting ground to another.

The only thing is, we hunt power instead of animals. We hunt light. We hunt perfection. We hunt oneness. We are that.

So the tribe has to be economically self-sufficient because we live in a world where money determines accessibility or inaccessibility. It is my suggestion that if you are part of the tribe, be it a neighboring tribe or the tribe in which I am, then you create economic resources for yourself and other members of your tribe.

And you do so through those mediums that I suggested, unless another comes more naturally to you, and that is through the electronic world or through the computer plane.

It's a natural for you; you've done it in many lives. You have power there; you've stored power there—through medicine, through the practice of law or through entertainment. These are arts that you have all practiced before. They'll come back to you.

If you have another inclination, explore it, certainly.

But it's very important for the coming times, which are going to be much rockier than even the good old year 1985 from which I am currently in temporal time speaking, to have a sound economic base and to be as mobile as possible.

To create a job, where, as the energy lines shift—because they'll be shifting in the coming times so strongly as we enter into the end phase of the Earth's cycle—that you can move from one place to another, that the tribe can move.

The economics is important because obviously, if one has enough money, it's possible to—in a society that runs by money, and status is, you know, achieved through money, and so on and so forth—it's obviously possible to buy the places that are necessary to live in relative inaccessibility and seclusion. Or to move with a bit of style and chicness into the middle of the civilization—whatever is called for.

I suggest for most of you, of course, computers. Because as a computer group we can move anywhere in the world and telecommunicate our work wherever we go.

Not simply to get a job in the field but to explore it, to see its power, to understand it. What we see being done in computers today is primitive—the hardware, but particularly the software.

And the software is the strength of the tribe because it's networking. It's creating oneness. It's creating tributaries that link together into a singular river.

The electronic tribe. As you work together, as you meet together, as you meditate together, you're going to create something rather perfect.

And that perfect thing is your attention—with a realistic appraisal of the conditions in the world and the darkness that we're in and that which is to come, which I assure you, will be even darker.

It's necessary to have a strong base, as strong a base as possible.

We've done this before in other worlds, in other lives. It is our strength—law, medicine, entertainment, computers.

Energy—the networking of energy, the expression of energy for healing; for order and administration, to create a sense of justice, of equality; simply for the pure joy of expression, the creative arts—singing, dancing, music; the plastic arts; the art of computers, or another art.

All of these things are arts—medicine, law, computers, electronics, entertainment—because art is the highest creation of energy.

Life itself is art, and the electronic tribe is a tribe of roving artists who are psychically connected and bonded with one purpose—oneness. To create such a perfect oneness that once again the body is one, the mind is one, the spirit is one.

Yet each retains a kind of especially ridiculous individuality, which makes it fun.

We will not be in this world much longer. We will be going someplace else.

So it's necessary to use your time as constructively as possible, to reach the totality, to become as aware as you can, of that which you really are. Not to waste your time. Not to be petty.

So I suggest that you look at your friends, at your tribal members, in a new way and you begin to understand the etiquette within the tribe and how it works.

The tribe is home. There is no place, physical place, that's home. Home is the tribe as it roams from place to place. That's the only home there is.

As a network, we roam the universes, the galaxies, the inter-dimensional planes. And we make friends wherever we go—because we're warriors of light, warriors of intensity, warriors of power.

To learn the ways of the occult and the psychic and the spiritual is your purpose. To remember. It's really not so much anything you have to learn as to remember where you've been and what you've done before and who you are. Who are you?

To engage yourself in work without seeking results, but just to bring your art to perfection, to create a strong economic base and to have a hell of a good time doing it because joy is the natural by-product of creativity, when creativity is done without attachment to results.

The wind is blowing. I'm here on the island of Nantucket. And the world is spinning, and we're all spinning with it.

And I can only hope that you're having as great a time with your life as I am with mine.

Because we're connected, all of us, we're one. Don't think of yourself as separate from me or from any other member of the tribe. Stop trying to be different.

Just do what you're good at, and work really hard. You have to work hard to be chaos, you know. The universe has a lot of practice at it.

And there's music in everything, and everything is a dance. So why not join in? Why just sit there by yourself—boo-hoo—when there's nothing but love and nothing but light and enlightenment?

Enlightenment. Never settle for anything else. Accept no substitutes. Make sure you read the ingredients first though, on the back of the label.

To make sure you really want it—ecstasy, perfection, awareness, caring, concern, love, fun, chaos—no singular system of order to content you or give you reasonable reasons for reasonable things that reasonably happen or don't happen. Ridiculous.

Ridiculous, this thing, and perfect. Enjoy it. Don't try and form it so much.

So as we gaze out into the twenty-first century, as we look into history—the future is history. It's what's already been—we're just going backwards in time again. We threw the wrong switch. Where are we now? There goes Napoleon, my God—Julius Caesar, Czar Kwangifim—the future, it's past! There's no time or space and this is hardly a Porsche and I'm hardly on Nantucket. All the usual pleasantries have been abolished.

There's only the tribe as it winds its way from universe to universe, from galaxy to galaxy, holding itself together through perfection.

That's our communication, is perfection.

So wherever you are, then here I am! And wherever I am, then here you are. And my brothers and sisters in the network and other worlds and other universes, well, wherever they are, there I am, and wherever I am, there they are.

Because we're connected. You get it—it's not so hard to figure out. Be easy!

Let go a little. Enjoy the show. I mean, we're all in this thing together, you know, and united we stand, and united we dissolve.

So the next time you're in the desert or walking through a shopping mall or buying a new car, trying on pants, getting that satin black blouse or having lunch with relatives, remember that you're part of the network, and the network is everywhere.

And as you're sitting there saying you like the way that blouse feels and looks, or passing the tuna fish to your cousin Eleanor, or passing your bar exam, or writing that program, or appearing on television talking about your latest film, or playing that music—remember the network.

Wherever you are, there they are. You can't be alone. It's terrible! You just can't get any peace. They're always there! All of them. Enlightenment. Endless life, stretching through everything. It's just hard to take sometimes. It's impossible to leave.

You understand—that's all that matters. So stop fighting. It's not suggestive of enlightenment. Stop feuding. Stop being jealous.

I mean, to be jealous is to suggest that God doesn't know what She's doing. To be jealous is, well, you want something that you don't have or someone that you don't have, or to be someplace that you aren't, but this is ridiculous! I mean, She does everything perfectly.

So you're exactly where you're supposed to be, and you have what you're supposed to have, and the worlds are spinning and colliding and dissolving and it's chaos, and it's wonderful and you're everywhere! And yet you're here!

The other members of the network understand your problems. [Rama laughs.]

There is only enlightenment. This is just a dream. And the music goes on and on—into eternity.

As Krishna once said to Arjuna in a similar situation, "Consider the past and future with an equal mind, and pass the Peanut M&M's."

So this is Rama. Everywhere.

Wishing you well. What more could I do, but to wish you well? Smile with me, and wish others well. The network makes friends wherever it goes because we smile and we wish everybody well.

And we stay out of places that are not appropriate for us. Neighborhoods. You know what I mean—intergalactic systems, dimensional planes—but wherever we go, we make friends. If you're not making friends, then you're not on the net.

I wish you well, my friends.   3-25-25

What if there is nothing to learn, only to remember? An exit, a memory out of the Eternal Return? Plans for navigating the second death? New-old friends are invited to visit. . . .

Warriorinitiate.COM

CHAPTER FIVE

KUNDALINI YOGA

It's 5:15 in the afternoon. I'm on the top of the world, 10,000 feet in Hawaii, on top of the Haleakala volcano.

The clouds have filled in all around it. I'm just above the cloud line, somewhere near the House of the Sun. Strange and unusual rocks are all around me—lava rocks, filled with power and energy.

The shadows are forming. The sun is dropping quickly over the horizon. As far as I can see are seas and oceans of cloud shapes and forms. Most of the island is obscured today, the lower island, by the clouds.

It's the first day of August in 1985, and I'm somewhere here in the middle of eternity.

I'd like to talk to you today about kundalini yoga, the yoga of power and energy.

The volcano is the symbol of power. This particular volcano is dormant at the moment—it's still. But within its depths the lava sits waiting, the power of the Earth.

And in a moment, lava will shoot forward, rise up through the lava tubes to the top of the volcano and erupt—the power within us that's dormant and the power of the universe that sits there waiting. Something happens—something triggers it—it goes off.

And it rises—it rises up the shushumna, the spinal astral tube. It gradually moves up through the chakras, and it reaches the thousand-petaled lotus of light at the top—enlightenment, satori, states of attention, perfection.

We are beautiful. We are beauty itself. We are visions of light, snapshots of eternity. Yet so few people in any given lifetime climb to the highest heights, experience the totality.

The path of kundalini yoga is the path of eruption, sudden spurts of energy—as you can hear in the background, the wind is blowing up here at 10,000 feet. And there's a wind that flows in and through your life, changing you.

The wind of time ages us. The wind of life changes its direction constantly.

But there is one constant in life, and that is the energy within your being.

How do you tap into it? How do you reach it? What will it do to you? How will it change you?

Is it dangerous? Can it be controlled? Or like these great volcanoes, is it something beyond our control and we can only watch with awe when the Earth displays itself?

It's funny how human beings tend to think that they're the masters of the Earth because they've put in a lot of shopping malls and painted little white lines on blacktop, never realizing that the Earth for a time simply tolerates its tenants and then, when the mood strikes, that it changes. It shifts its continents around. Mountains rise and fall.

We take so much for granted.

Kundalini yoga is the yoga of transmutation. The principles are simple.

At the base of the spine there's an access point that leads into another world, another plane of attention, another dimension.

It's possible to access the energy through that secret doorway, that lowest chakra, and bring that energy and power up through yourself into your being. And as you bring it into your being, it will spread and radiate throughout your entire body.

There is a particular path that the kundalini follows—the shushumna. The shushumna, as I mentioned before, is an astral nerve tube. It's the central nerve tube. There are two others, the ida and the pingala, on either side of it.

In most persons, the shushumna is closed. It's a highway that's been shut down. The continuous energy flow that gives us life, that sustains the subtle physical body, takes place in the ida and the pingala.

Just as the blood is constantly flowing through your veins through capillaries—bringing oxygen to the cells, moving nutrients and wastes around—so the kundalini energy is constantly flowing through our subtle physical body, our etheric body.

It sustains it, heals it. Without that energy, the subtle body grows ill, gets injured or it dies. And when it dies, the physical body dies.

We are completely dependent upon the subtle physical body in this world.

The more energy that we have in the subtle physical body, the higher our psychic receptivity is.

So kundalini yoga is, in many ways, the study of energy—its management, its flow, its highs and its lows. But specifically, kundalini is a flow of power.

And when we diagram it, we say that it runs from the base of the spine up to the top of the head.

Now, it isn't exactly running in the physical body, of course. Kundalini is running through the subtle physical. The subtle physical looks approximately like the physical body, only it's composed of thousands of layers of light, light fibers.

It is knowledge itself.

The subtle physical body conducts light the same way that a piece of wire conducts electricity. But it also reflects light the way a mirror reflects a visage, a scene.

There are seven chakras, gateways to the kundalini.

- ॐ There is one at the base of the spine.
- ॐ There is one halfway between the base of the spine and the navel.
- ॐ There is a chakra at the navel.
- ॐ There is a chakra in the center of the chest, at about the elevation of the heart.
- ॐ There is a chakra in the area of the throat, the lower throat, where the neck joins to the torso.
- ॐ There is a chakra between the eyebrows and slightly above—the third eye.
- ॐ And there's a chakra at the top of the head—the crown chakra.

The lower six chakras are connected by the shushumna, the ida and the pingala. The crown chakra is not connected to the other six—it's separate.

Each of the chakras, of course, has been described in yogic literature as being formed of lotuses or petals. A different number of petals have been assigned to each of the chakras and a different symbolic color, and so on.

What really concerns the student is not so much the number of petals or the colors or the plane of attention that a certain chakra is associated with, but rather, it's the simple shifting of energy—how to pull and move the kundalini up the shushumna through each chakra and eventually how to make that jump, from the third eye to the thousand-petaled lotus, to the crown chakra on the top of the head.

A cautionary note—kundalini yoga, unlike some types of yoga, tends to be a little more dangerous—dangerous if it is not practiced correctly. When practiced correctly, there's no danger at all.

But to prematurely push the kundalini energy through the chakras can cause a variety of ailments, the most common of which is insanity.

What is insanity?

> Insanity is the inability to confine perception to a particular plane of attention.

So for example, when a person is practicing kundalini yoga, if they were to push their attention too far too fast, they can gain visions of other worlds. These visions can be enlightening, beautific, or terribly frightening, depending upon the nature of the vision, and, of course, the individual's own reactions to it. I mean, nothing is really beautiful or fearful until we decide that it is.

Also, there are various beings that live in other planes of attention that one will see and encounter in alternate realities.

Needless to say, if a person is properly prepared, it's simply like journeying to a foreign land. In the foreign land, we will experience another culture, another language, different social customs, religions, different types of people. And we're not particularly thrown if we've been a little oriented to what we're going to experience. It can be exciting. We can learn a lot.

How much are you learning lately? Are you learning enough?

Have you learned that you're not a body composed of cells and tissues?

Have you learned that this world, as you know it, doesn't even exist? Do you know that there is not a beginning or an ending? That there is no today or tomorrow?

That all of the relative appearances that you see don't really exist as you think they do?

The kundalini gives this knowledge and awareness. It frees you. It frees you from duality, the sense of right and wrong, good and bad, love and hate, beauty and ugliness, winning and losing.

Everything depends upon perception. We are perception.

Kundalini is an alteration of perception.

I try to describe kundalini in a schematic sense, saying that there are chakras and that there is an energy flow, and so on. And it's true, it's true, it's true, it's true, it's true, it's true, it's sort of—it's not completely true.

Nothing is completely true. Nothing that can be expressed is completely true because anything that can be expressed is a partiality, and yet, something can be transmitted—awareness—awareness of eternity. That's all there is.

I'm here at 10,000 feet on the island of Maui. The clouds are moving and shifting beneath me—huge billowy clouds. And so our lives shift. The characters in our lives come and go. Our emotions—fleeting, beautiful, agonizing.

Kundalini is control. Perfect control. Control of everything, from within.

Most individuals try to control their lives from outside of themselves. They seek to influence and affect their environment. So human beings have shaped the world to fit their own image.

Yoga, kundalini yoga, is the science of shaping attention, awareness. We are not so concerned about the world around us, as we are the world within us because we realize that the world within us is the world around us.

Every perception we have, everything we see, feel and experience is dependent upon our state of mind. Mind is relative. It changes constantly.

Control of mind is control of destiny, control of life, control of awareness.

Control of mind is not gained simply by battling desires, but rather it's gained through energy.

Energy is awareness. Awareness is attention. Attention is purpose. Purpose is ... endless.

Let's get practical. You are in a certain state of consciousness right now.

The state of consciousness that you're in causes you to enjoy your life or to not enjoy your life—to see the beauty in things and people or not to see that beauty, to succeed in work or not to succeed in work, to be loved and to love, to be hated, to be feared, to be fearful—everything is dependent upon your state of awareness. It colors the universe.

Your state of awareness is dependent upon the kundalini flow within yourself.

Most individuals, in order to become happy, feel that they can fulfill desires. That will make them happy. So you'll get the car, the person, the experience, the money, the vacation, whatever it might be, and that's going to make you happy.

But if you're not in the right state of consciousness, you won't be happy.

Remember—wherever you go, there you are. You take yourself with you when you travel.

And if your state of attention is not very high, then whatever you see, whatever you experience, whatever wonders are presented to your eyes, you will experience those things only to the extent that your attention—your level of awareness—allows.

If you have infinite, endless awareness, then the most miserable conditions as defined by others can be the most wonderful.

Poverty is not poverty, wealth is not wealth, illness is not illness and health is not health. No longer are you subject to the relative conditions of the world.

In other words, the interpretations that most people place upon things—this makes you happy, this makes you unhappy—no longer applies to you.

Because your apprehension of the cosmos is completely changed—it's shifted—not just once to another vantage point, but it becomes a mirror image of the cosmos itself. It constantly shifts and changes.

There is no such thing as reality. There is no singular defining code. Access to the kundalini changes attention, changes awareness.

Beyond happiness and unhappiness is truth. Truth is not affected by anything in the relative world.

Truth is the unifying aspect of existence. Truth is not a truth, meaning that there is one thing that can be said that will give us an answer or the answer.

Rather, truth is the very substance of life itself.

But very few people perceive or feel that substance. We don't know what it is. Or perhaps we've had a glimpse of it—the most wonderful thing—but we don't know how to reach it, not realizing that there's nothing to reach.

That it is our very self, our very awareness, that is the window upon which reality ... presents ... itself.

We are our awareness—a seemingly simple statement.

Meditation—stopping thought for protracted periods of time—shifts our awareness.

When there's no thought, the kundalini rises. When there's thought, the kundalini is inactive. When you create a vacuum, something will be drawn into it. When you stop thought, the kundalini is drawn into your attention field. The less thought you have, the more the kundalini will flow through the chakras, through the shushumna.

To reduce thought is not simply a process of learning a technique, repeating a mantram, eating the right kind of breakfast cereal, crossing at the green and not in between. Stopping thought isn't simply a disciplined practice.

Stopping thought also involves shifting your values.

You see, thought is stimulated by ideas that we have about life in the world. These ideas were given to us by our culture, our society. We were imprinted with a value system as young children, and simply the sensory experiences of life can trigger and stimulate a variety of associative thoughts and ideas.

In order to lessen our thoughts and therefore to increase the flow of kundalini—which will alter our perception and give us a larger view or vision of life itself, and freedom and happiness in the face of any circumstances—it's necessary to clarify the purpose of our being.

This is to come to understand dharma.

Dharma is a Sanskrit word. It simply means that which is right, that which is correct, that which is the divine law.

It is necessary first, in the practice of kundalini yoga, to determine what the dharma is.

There is a dharma for yourself, for someone else, for a family, for a nation, for a planet, for a universe. There are collective dharmas and individual dharmas.

Your dharma is what kind of work you should be doing, what kind of people you should associate with, whether you should be practicing meditation or not. If so, what type? Whether you should have a teacher or not. If so, what type?

How you should see the world, how much you should give selflessly, how much of your money you should donate to spiritual activities, how much of your time you should donate to selfless giving and aiding others, how much of your time you should spend by yourself and alone and in a reclusive mode, how much of your time you should just have a tremendous amount of fun and just be frivolous and silly, whether you should be reverential and follow the path of the heart.

Dharma encompasses all things.

And it's specific to the individual.

So the first task is to discover the dharma, and this is done through introspection, by continually questioning yourself and asking yourself, "What is the right thing for me to do? Not simply the thing I want. Not simply avoiding the thing I don't want. What is right?"

Because to not follow dharma leads to disaster. Life will be unhappy.

Following dharma puts you in a proper field of attention, and in a proper field of attention; regardless of what your outer circumstances are, happiness will flow.

To not follow the dharma—either intentionally or through lack of awareness—creates a very low level of attention, and in this low level of attention, we make all kinds of mistakes and we're unhappy, no matter what good fortune apparently befalls us.

You will be unhappy if you do not follow the dharma.

Happiness does not come from external objects. It comes from peace of mind.

You can have one hundred Rolls Royces, you can have everyone devoted to you, you can have people who love you, you can be famous, you can be a king, a queen, anything. But it does not necessarily bring happiness or peace of mind.

Happiness and peace of mind is a very, very beautiful and simple thing. And it comes about through following dharma.

Naturally, to follow dharma, we have to first find out what it is. So you ask yourself continually, in every situation and also in the larger context of life, "What is the right thing for me to do?"

And you have to struggle with it. You have to fight with it to find out. The answer will not come easily. You will be swayed by your desires, by your conditioning, the things that you've been taught to do or to avoid. You will be swayed by those around you who have ideas about what you should do, what is proper, what is improper.

All of these thoughts and feelings will affect you.

But if you're determined, if you won't give in, if you're joyous, if you truly want to celebrate life, then you will persist in discovering dharma. No matter what apparent obstacles appear before you, you'll laugh your way through them, or you'll work your way through them, or you'll glide through them. Whatever is necessary, you will do.

The answer then, is love. Love is the bridge that joins all of the worlds together. Love permits us to see who and what we are.

The only thing that will truly inspire us to find the dharma—to find the wonderful path that leads us to awareness—is love.

Only love will give us that strength. Love is something that comes to us in life. Quietly, it overwhelms us. It is something that you cultivate. You make it happen.

The kundalini flows upward. It also flows downward in different ways. It is quite complex, actually. What is most important, though, is to have your life properly aligned with dharma. The technicalities of the movement of the kundalini are easy to master.

Dharma is much more complex, and if the kundalini is flowing through you at a very rapid rate when you practice kundalini yoga, if you are not in harmony with the dharma, then you will have great problems with the study.

This is the principle thing that I have seen.

And that's that people want power ... but not wisdom. Power without wisdom is a very dangerous thing. Better to find wisdom first. Certainly, a certain amount of power is required to live, to exist in the world.

But without wisdom, power tends to destroy the one who wields it.

Kundalini yoga is the yoga of power.

Wisdom comes from introspection. It comes from caring, it comes from sharing. And with wisdom, the powerful person will become more powerful. There is no end to power. There is no end to love or knowledge.

Without wisdom—without a sense of place in the universe, of that which is apropos and that which is not—then a powerful person does not become more powerful. Their power will turn back on them and eventually destroy them.

So those who are truly wise become most powerful.

Those who are not wise squander their power on useless and trivial things—they waste it. And very often they injure others or themselves.

So from my point of view, kundalini yoga then depends upon a sense of dharma, a sense of that which is right.

That which is right is different for each one of us in each situation.

There isn't a moral code that I or anyone else can lay down that will tell you what your dharma is.

But there is a simple way to know when you are following it.

When you are following dharma ... you'll be happy, at peace, still inside. There will be a sense of purpose in your life. Your life will go well. Difficulties will not seem unconquerable.

When you're not following dharma, then you will not be at peace. You will not be happy. The simplest things will seem to be endless obstacles.

It is not what we do, it's who we are. And who we are varies according to our awareness. When you're more aware, you're someone else than when you're less aware.

Right now I'm above the clouds at 10,000 feet, and I can see the blue sky, and I can see for miles and miles.

Down underneath those clouds the people of Maui live, and today they are not having a sunny day. The clouds have rolled in. There is not too much light down there, and I'm up here on top of the mountain and there's nothing but light and blue sky. The clouds are desires. The clouds are our loves, our fears, our world, our ideas, ideals. These are the clouds.

You can climb above the clouds to freedom, or you can stay beneath them in darkness. It's up to you.

The kundalini will take you up above the clouds. It will give you a quick vision of your own immortality, the most wondrous and perfect thing there is.

But to stay here, to live in this condition of eternality endlessly, which is what, of course, we call enlightenment, is the goal of kundalini yoga—or any yoga, or any path that leads to self-knowledge.

The glimpse tells us that it's possible that there is such a world. And I believe that in each one of our lives there are days like that. There are days when life is clear and simple, when we feel the intimations of immortality.

It has been my experience as a teacher over the years and incarnations, let alone as a student, that what really counts are not techniques.

What really counts is spirit—love. What really counts is a sense of propriety and dedication. These are the qualities that manifest in self-realization.

The kundalini varies, not simply through breathing techniques or by meditating on chakras, but by stopping thought.

To stop thought it's necessary to put your life into a state of balance. Otherwise you can sit and meditate for hours and hours and all kinds of conscious and subconscious thoughts will flow through you.

It is possible with pure willpower to force the kundalini up the shushumna, through the chakras. Then, as I indicated before, you will develop visions of other worlds, but these visions will not necessarily stop or go away when you want them to.

This is a condition that we call insanity, when you cannot clear perceptual fields. It's like watching 20 stations on television at once, and after a while, you can't tell which is the right one. This is what happens to individuals who force—who push—the kundalini out too far without having the balance.

When you have the balance, it's not a problem—it's a snap. Then you can easily segment the realities, when your attention field is fluid.

But to develop that fluidity, it's necessary to follow the dharma.

So my recommendation is—if you seek to practice kundalini yoga—to meditate, of course, and you can meditate on the different chakras and feel what that's like.

But what will really release the kundalini is something much simpler and more effective—in addition to meditation techniques, breathing techniques, and so on.

And that's by creating a stillness in your life. This stillness will come about through deep caring and introspection. It will come about slowly, and then quickly. It builds in momentum.

Begin with your daily life.

Take your life as a challenge and try to bring yourself into harmony with each thing in your life—with your occupation, with your relationship with nature and the Earth. Bring yourself into harmony with your friends, your family, your country.

Harmony sometimes means withdrawal. Sometimes it means leaving those you love for something that you love more. Sometimes it means duty. It means so many different things.

You'll have to go through a trial-and-error process, but you will always know when there's a deeper stillness in your daily meditation, a deeper stillness in your life. That means that what you're doing is working.

And if you're not finding that—if you're exhausted all the time and hassled and you just can't meditate well at all, it means that your priorities are all fouled up … and you need to shift them around.

So sit down and get out a piece of paper and start making lists. Make lists of everyone who's important to you, everything that's important to you, everything that you desire, everything that you fear.

Flowchart your life. Go through it. It is good to do this every few months.

And ask yourself, are you in harmony with the things in your life? Or are you adopting superficial values which really are not the real you? Are you giving your being enough room? Are you doing enough new and creative and exciting things?

Dharma doesn't necessarily mean following a mundane and boring life. It means a life of high adventure. It means a life of newness, not a life of endless, boring repetition.

So doing the dharma may be doing very new things, meeting new people, going on new adventures, meditating in new ways.

The sign that the kundalini is releasing is not the development of miraculous powers, but it's the fact that your mind is becoming quieter, that there's an interior stillness.

Very often, strangely enough, in order to bring about the interior stillness we have to be tirelessly active in the outer world. We've got to go out and go on a quest, go on a journey, accomplish things, do things.

Now, normally you might suppose that this would agitate the mind and create a lack of stillness. But it will not, if it's the dharma. What we do outwardly will only interrupt the flow of our perfect attention if it's not in harmony with the dharma.

So if it's right for you to travel across the world to go on a great journey, if that's what the dharma is, if you've correctly perceived it, then those actions will actually bring a stillness into your life. Whereas, if you try to start a giant corporation, and if that's not the dharma, then it will only bring agitation in your life.

On the other hand, for you to work in or start a corporation—instead of taking that wonderful, happy journey that might seem more attractive—might be the dharma. If you go on that journey, then you'll just become more and more miserable, whereas every day you go to work and do nine to five, that may bring about a stillness in your life.

It's specific to the individual and it can change for you.

What can be the dharma at one point in your life can totally reverse itself, and suddenly you might be doing the opposite or something very new, something you never considered.

You find out by meditating, by stilling your thoughts, by bringing about a balance in your life, by feeling deeply, by asking questions constantly. What is right? What does the universe want me to do?

And then, once you determine that and you're sure, you need to go about it with style, with a little bit of excitement, with bravado, with adventure, with stoicism.

All adventures in life will bring about a mixture of pleasure and pain and loss and gain.

But these things don't matter because when you're following the dharma, you're operating on an entirely different reference frame.

Success is not success in an individual endeavor. Success is simply to practice the dharma impeccably. Then the kundalini will flow. Then your awareness will shift. Then your meditation will be wonderful.

If your meditation is frustrating, if it's not happening, and it was at one time good and exciting in your life and you're putting in the same number of minutes, then that was because during that time in your life you were following the dharma more.

You had felt it, and you were following it in your daily life, in your daily thoughts.

If that's not happening now, then it means you've got to shift what you're doing. You've got to get creative with your lifestyle.

Change your job, change your friends, change the place you live. Change your goals, change your attitudes. Work harder, work less. Travel. Don't travel. You've got to mix it up.

And if you keep trying with that intent, then eventually you will stumble upon—or be guided to—that which will bring about the highest good, the highest stillness.

Then the kundalini in your daily meditations will release. This is my experience. Don't worry about techniques. Don't worry about chakras. Instead, concern yourself with finding the dharma and meditate.

Then the kundalini will release.

This is real kundalini yoga, not simply a series of repetitive exercises and movements that you could practice for hundreds of years and never substantially open up the fields of kundalini energy and have them release into your being.

The release comes about through a balanced life, and, of course, through periods of formal and informal meditation.

Through association with other higher beings, with a teacher, with people along the path, with nonphysical beings—whatever works, do it.

That's what makes it exciting and fun.

And then life is wonderful. It's terrific. It's jazzy.

And still, there will be obstacles, of course. Still there will be adventure, of course. Your life is your life, and each thing will be a challenge. But the movement of life will be flowing with you. You will be in harmony with the Tao, with the basic principles of creation.

To not be in harmony with that flow, no matter how hard you meditate, no matter how hard you strive to attain liberation, you will not be happy, and you won't be liberated.

Because you did everything but the most important thing—bring about stillness in your life.

Have some fun with it. Be creative with consciousness. Be sensitive to what's above the clouds and below them and to the clouds themselves.

Maui is a beautiful island.

It's really the site of an ancient civilization that we've forgotten about, a civilization that existed millions of years ago. There was a continent here then, and a group of highly developed psychic beings lived here, and they brought about a terrific harmony in their lives. They followed dharma.

And then, when their time came, they left this world and another race was born, the race of human beings.

Human beings are not so in harmony with the dharma. That's why they suffer so much.

But you as an individual can reach a higher plane of attention, can become attention itself.

So start simply every day by asking yourself, "What is the dharma today? What should I do? What is right? What does the universe want from me?" Find a beauty in that, a balance. Then look at your whole life, and say, "Is this what I should be doing now? It was fine before, is it still fine?"

Do a systems analysis of your life. Balance it.

And meditate for about two hours a day—an hour in the morning and an hour in the evening. If you're new, perhaps a half an hour twice a day. Enter into that stillness.

Try and stop your thoughts. Be patient. And then the kundalini will flow through you and bring about substantial changes in your awareness.

The future is certain for those who follow dharma. The future is endless existence.

Those who don't follow dharma are pushed back again and again into the net of rebirth. They are drawn back to the same planes of attention, or lower. It could happen to you!

So look for the still point between the worlds. Find it in your own smile. Look in your eyes in a mirror. And ask yourself, "What is the dharma? What is it that I should be doing?" And don't be afraid to do it.

Death teaches us not to be afraid because we know it will come to us, and we'll deal with it effectively. We have for thousands of times, so what is there to fear?

We are immortal life. Instead, think of the opportunity of self-realization. What a gas!

From Haleakala at 10,000 feet, I wish you and your kundalini well.

Later.

CHAPTER SIX

POWER

Hello power lovers. I am here today on top of the Continental Divide, 11,500 feet up above the earth. I'm parked by the side of the road. It's around 7:45 in the evening on August 7th. Occasionally a car or truck will roar by.

I'm facing some distant power mountains—a suitable place to discuss with you the end of the world.

The world has an ending and a beginning. It begins with you and it ends with you.

The end of this world occurs when you make a major transition in attention—when you move from one world into another, from one reality into another.

Everything is dependent upon energy.

Energy is attention.

Attention is awareness.

You were born with a specific amount of energy. That energy came from "the totality." It came from your other lives. In this lifetime, you can increase your energy or you can decrease it.

Mysticism is the study of energy, the study of power—its use, its abuse. At every moment you are getting stronger or you are growing weaker. At every moment your attention field is increasing or it is decreasing.

Why? Why have energy? Why have power? Does it matter? Is it spiritual?

The more energy you have, the more freedom you have. In the physical world, money is freedom. If you have money, if you have wealth, then you can do what you want. You can get on a plane and go anyplace in the world. You can live wherever you want to, and no one will bother you. If they do, you can hire people to aid you.

Without money, you're powerless in this world. You can't buy food, you can't travel—you're totally subject to whatever happens. If someone says that you've broken the law and if you don't have money for a good attorney, you may go to jail—even if you didn't do something wrong. If you have money for a good attorney, you may go free—even if you did do something wrong.

Money is not inviolable. It doesn't change all conditions. But to be without money from the strategic point of view in the physical world is to be powerless.

In the inner world, it's the same, only it's pure power. Power is the ability to translate, that is, to shift from one level of attention to another.

Right now, you're in a certain strata of awareness. Your awareness, your happiness, your unhappiness, all of these conditions are largely based upon your ability to move your attention.

If you stay in the attention you're in, then you can predict everything that will happen to you for the rest of your life—your happinesses, your unhappinesses, your successes and your failures.

You are in a country. In the country, the most you'll ever make in dollars and cents is fixed. You can't rise above it. The nicest house you can ever live in in that country, the nicest home, is whatever the nicest home is within that country. You can't rise above it. The worst thing that can ever happen to you in that country is the worst thing that ever happens to anyone in that country. This is attention.

Attention is life. Attention, or the lack of it, is death.

Right now you're in a country. The country is your mind.

Your mind is filled with thoughts, desires, aspirations, loves, hates, jealousies, pure feelings. They constantly change and shift around you. You are in a jungle and there are many creatures roaming through it. You are subject to those creatures.

Freedom is within oneself. But how to get beyond the thoughts, the desires? How to get into a different country? That requires power.

You have a certain amount of power. You were born with it. That power created the country that you now reside in. Your power comes from the totality, from the absolute reality, from God—whatever you'd like to call infiniteness.

But now you're here, and that's all that matters. What's gone before is gone. All you have now are the results of your actions. At this moment, you are as powerful as you are. You are no more or no less powerful than you are.

At this moment, you can measure your power in your ability to stop thought. The longer you can stop thought, the more powerful you are. When you stop thought, you shift planes of reality, you move from one country into another. If you can only do it for a short period of time, then you can only reside in those more beautiful lands for short periods of time.

The longer you can suspend thought, the more permanent the shifts inside yourself, in your awareness. Not only for those moments in which there is no thought but for those moments after, for those days, those weeks, for that life and for the next life.

When thought stops, power increases.

There are many ways to store power. You can visit places of power, special locations on the Earth that are charged with power. You can be around powerful people. You can read the writings, listen to the tapes or read about beings of power.

In other words, anything that puts you in touch with power—exercise, certain types of food, fasting, breaking up routines, specific ways of dreaming, certain ways of looking at life—there are many, many ways to shift one's attention, to be more or less powerful.

Does power bring happiness? Does it bring refinement? Does it bring humor? Does it bring a good-heartedness, or is it just cold? Power is never cold. Cold people may use power in cold ways, but power itself is simply a word to try and describe attention, awareness, which embodies all things.

If you have only been around people who use power in cruel and petty ways, then when you hear the very word, you may have a negative reaction.

But it's important to redefine that word. It doesn't mean anything in particular. It can mean anything that you want it to. It can mean anything whatsoever.

Power. Power is what's required to change the universe—to change yourself into what you might like to be.

If a rocket seeks to put a space ship, a satellite, whatever it may be, into orbit, it has to have power. The more velocity it has, the higher the orbit will be of the satellite or the space station or the space ship.

A great deal of power is required to go above the Earth's gravitational field. If there's enough power, then an orbit is gained above the Earth, above the world. Eventually gravity will pull the object back down. The higher the orbit, the longer it will take.

If there's enough power, then one can break free of the Earth's gravity field. But then again, one could get trapped in the field of another heavenly body, so to speak.

So it's necessary then to store power to be free.

Right now you're in the gravity field of many different people who are in your life. Each person you feel attached to is a planetary body—perhaps a heavenly body—that is exerting a certain force in your life, and in order to be free you need not attraction or repulsion—you need power.

That way, you can pass through this world, through the cosmos, and enjoy the universe but not be trapped by the gravity fields of others.

Power. Unadulterated pure power.

There's an art, naturally, or a science, or both—maybe it's the same—to gaining power. And to be honest with you, there's a natural force or inclination in all of our beings to accumulate power.

The problem that we come into is conditioning—our own conditioning and the conditioning of others.

Now listen carefully. This sounds simple but it's very complex. It runs deep into the psyche.

When you were born, you were free. Your attention field, your awareness is not yet formed. Your attention field is the sum total of your experiences from other lives, yes, but yet, it is not conditioned. It is not fully manifested as a seed.

Within the seed is the tree. Yet if we know seeds, we can look at a particular seed and say, "This will grow into an apple tree, this will grow into an oak tree, this will grow into an orange tree." The entire tree is contained in the seed. Some seeds will never germinate. But if the proper conditions are provided, they will.

So, when you were born, you were a seed.

You were the seed of your past experiences and actions in other theaters of existence, in other worlds, in other lives. Those lives are gone, for all intents and purposes. But yet, you are the seed, and if the seed is planted in the right ground, it will grow.

And one who can see can look at a child and say, "Yes, I can see the evolution of this child and what this child will grow into when it is mature." The child may not outwardly evidence any of those traits or characteristics yet, but one who sees looks through the physical and temporal and can tell you the potential of a child.

Well, of course, I do the same thing.

As a seer, I naturally can see the evolutionary potential of a being. But the potential will not necessarily be actualized. A particular being will not necessarily realize their full height.

If we plant an orange tree in a cold climate, it won't grow. Or it will grow for a while and then die. If we plant a tree in too much shade, if there are other big trees around it and it doesn't get enough light, it will grow, but it may never bear fruit. So conditions are important, conditioning.

Conditioning comes from parents and the adults or others around the child. The child is born with a potential in seed form. The conditions, though, are not so much the geographical areas but the people, the luminous beings, who surround the child.

Each person has an attention field. Their attention field is the sum total of their awareness and their imprinting.

There is normally, in the life of each child, a dominant male and dominant female—usually the physical mother or father. It could be the adopted mother or father; it could be anyone. In other words, the male or female that the child has the most exposure to in the first four to six years of its life, particularly the first four, is the primary imprinter of the child. The imprinter of the child will condition the child.

Now, a child could have many, many imprinters in those first years. And of course, one is imprinted also in the following years, but the most serious imprinting occurs in those first years. So, lets say a child was raised in a commune and it was exposed to six or seven different men or six or seven different women. Then they would all be the imprinters, and the imprinting that the child's attention field took on would be the sum total of the different views. This is not better than having one imprinter, or worse. It depends on the individuals.

A child is imprinted not by simply the teaching, not by saying, "Johnny, this is a good action, and this is a bad action." Of course that's an obvious imprinting.

But attention is like soft, soft clay, a child's attention field. And the attention fields of adults, in particular, are stratified. They're like hard clay and they have different shapes, if you could see them inwardly.

So imagine that we have a young child, and the body is made of clay. It's very soft. Let's say we take one male and one female, and let's say that the male's shape is square and the female's shape is round. And let's say we take one, and we push them on each side of the child's attention field. And let's say that we push the round field of the woman on the left side of the child and the square field on the right side of the child.

And we push them in, and push them and push them, and we let them hold there until the clay of the child hardens. Then we back them off, and now the child will be imprinted.

In other words, nothing has to be said, nothing has to be explained. Just by being around the awareness field of the male or female imprinter, the child is imprinted. The child will also gain imprints, obviously, from others, and in later life—teachers, lovers, husbands, wives.

We continue to imprint throughout our lives, but the critical imprinting, the deepest imprinting, occurs in the first four years.

But the other imprinting that follows is also extremely significant. The first sexual experience, for example, is a significant imprinting.

Everyone imprints all the time and is imprinted because our consciousness is never completely hardened, but it becomes more stratified as we grow older, as more and more imprints are taken.

In mysticism, the first course of action is to do away with the imprinting. We have to take all the imprinting that's occurred to us in this life and wash it. We have to make ourselves soft again and push it all aside. Then, we need to be re-imprinted, but in a different way.

Imprinting is important. Without it, we don't survive. The child needs to be imprinted. It seeks it, as a matter of fact. It's essential. The child seeks to be imprinted because it has to have a way of dealing with the world, and those who imprint it obviously have managed to survive in this world.

Imprinting is critical.

If your parents were strong in one way and weak in another, you will be strong in the same way and weak in the same way. Even though you may detest the weakness that you saw in them, you will find that you will do exactly the same things in the same situation because they imprinted you. Not by choice. That is to say, they didn't want to give you a weak imprint. They might have wanted the opposite, but they couldn't help themselves. Perhaps they were imprinted in the same way.

We are all carrying the imprints of our most ancient ancestors. Not simply in the genetic code, in the DNA within us, but in the imprints of attention that are passed on.

There are also subtle imprints that occur in a society. A whole society imprints us; a language, a culture imprints us. Television. Just living in a country is a vibratory imprint. All the collective attentions of all the people who live there imprint us. Everybody's thinking the same thing, desiring the same things.

Even though we don't have physical contact with people, if we're within a certain geographical area, or even on a specific planet or in a certain dimensional plane, we are imprinted.

We ourselves are free attention. You are not anyone or anything in particular. You are attention itself. You are awareness itself. You don't have a particular form. You contain everything or everything is contained within you, or you are contained by all things.

So the mystic, one who studies the ways of power, seeks to end the imprinting process because in imprinting we lose power, we lose attention. We're formatted to do certain things. But obviously the people who imprinted us are not completely happy and they're not completely powerful.

If you lived in a world of completely powerful enlightened beings, then obviously you would have a clean imprint. But we don't. We live in a world filled with poverty, suffering, war and unhappiness and transitory joy. So naturally, we receive that imprint, and we have to fight our whole life against that imprinting.

But we need a new imprinting. We need the imprinting of enlightenment, of freedom. And that comes through our association with a higher being. So classically what occurs, is one meets a teacher—one who has knowledge.

And that being will teach you how to overcome your old imprinting by changing your way of life and by teaching you the ways of power—how to store it, collect it, amplify it, how to stop losing it. By bringing enough power into your life, you will gradually erase or actually overcome your imprinting.

And then the teacher will have a certain imprint, and each teacher imprints differently. They imprint according to their own characteristics.

Now still, even ultimately, to a certain extent, the imprint of the teacher is a limitation that you will finally have to overcome in your final stages of self-realization, of knowledge. You will go beyond the teacher's imprint.

But if you had a truly enlightened teacher, the dominant spiritual seeker that you came into contact with personally or inwardly, then they will give you a correct imprint and that correct imprint will aid you in your self-discovery. In the last stages, you will overcome it. But it won't be something that will hold you back. It will fall away naturally if it was a correct imprint.

If your parents, your physical parents, or whoever imprinted you were well balanced—if they were happy, if they had a good attitude about life, if they didn't try and hold on to you, to wrap you up, to make you feel guilty and all those things that most parents do—then they did you a favor. Their imprint is not necessarily bad.

It has to be transcended if you want to go into the other worlds of attention, if you want to be free. Because even at its best, it's still a limited description of the world, unless they themselves were mystics of a high order. Then even the best human imprint is still a human imprint, and it has to be gone beyond.

And it requires power to do this. Power will take us beyond the gravity field of the imprint.

So it's necessary, then, to do systems analysis of your life—to look at where you gain power, where you lose power, and to do the things that empower you and avoid the things that drain you.

And then it's necessary to seek out one who can re-imprint you.

Now, the re-imprinting process is really fascinating.

First of all, I'm making it sound a bit like you don't have to do the work, and that's not true at all. Because in order to draw a teacher, that is to say, one who will imprint you properly, you have to store quite a bit of power by leading a certain type of life, let's say.

Now once you have drawn such a teacher, it's another matter to be in the right state of attention for them to properly imprint you. Oh, imprint you they will. But as to how well that imprint will take, well, it depends a lot upon how much you have erased your original imprint.

No one can bring you into higher states of attention permanently. I can take an individual and I can change their awareness. That's easy. But how long will it last? Oh, there will be a residual positive effect. Whenever I'm in physical contact with someone, naturally, my attention field is obviously imprinting them in a certain way.

That's why just associating with a powerful person is obviously a good thing. But it won't necessarily create the substantial changes that are necessary for a person to spin themselves into other worlds—to go beyond the unhappiness and frustration of human experience and, in this life, to reach the totality of themselves and experience freedom and knowledge and fun.

No, each person has to do that on their own, just as I had to and continue to have to do it on me own. So a teacher can show you those ways. But no one can do it for you.

Then you have to take what you learn from them and go out and live it. You have to fight your battles of power. You have to overcome your own conditioning. You have to change your life.

Think of your life as a field. There's a big field beyond your house. And let's say that everything that you need comes from that field, and in that field you grow all the food you eat and you collect the water that you drink. Your life is dependent upon what comes in and out of that field.

Now, let's say that some people use their field well; some use it poorly.

The field is the field of action. You're born with a certain amount of luminosity; you're born with a certain amount of power, true. But in order for that luminosity and power to grow, you need a certain environmental condition.

So what the mystic does, is they set up their life as a field of power.

In other words, you can draw power from everything in your life, and that power will roll into your being. It will increase your own power and it will also trigger a reaction.

And that reaction will be the release of the power within yourself, just as when we split an atom—the tremendous power and energy released—matter converts into energy. So we can split the atom, the nucleus of our own being where all our power from all our lives is stored.

But in order to do that, everything has to be set up in a proper way.

Otherwise, either it won't work or the results will be catastrophic.

So it's necessary to groom our life, to bring it into order, to examine each thing in our life and ask ourselves if it's bringing power and force and energy into our life or if it's draining it. So it's necessary to look at each relationship we have, at our career, where we live, at our habits and routines, at our thought patterns. Each item has to be carefully gone through and constantly improved and checked and rechecked.

The question you have to ask yourself, the most basic question is, is your life taking power from you? Or is it adding power to you? You need an honest answer. Are you stronger each day?

When I say stronger, I don't simply mean your physical body, but is your awareness stronger? And remember, the way we measure awareness is by how long you can stop thought.

If you can't stop thought at all at this time, then you are not powerful. You might be quite evolved, but you have no access to that evolution. You've inherited money, but it hasn't come to you yet, and it might not come to you. It's necessary for you to stop thought.

So if then, as a guideline, you are finding that you can stop thought longer and longer—which means going to the higher levels of attention for longer and longer periods of time or timelessness—if you see that trend in your life, then I would say that your life is bringing power into your being. You're gaining things out from that field behind the house. You're growing vegetables and plants and you've got some buckets out to collect some water.

Now, how efficiently you're using the field that you have, how efficiently you're using the life situations around you, is a question. That's what we have to try and determine.

So then you move into the program of mysticism, of self-discovery, which is what I teach and some others teach. How to do that—how to increase the productivity.

On the other hand, your life may be draining away. Every day you may be getting older instead of younger, more frustrated instead of happier. Your job may not be progressing at the rate you would like it to. Your relationships may not be evolving. You may not be as happy as you once were. If you're not, then certainly your power is dwindling.

If you're happier than you've ever been, then it's increasing.

But is it as fast a rate of climb as you would like?

Obviously, if it's decreasing, then you've got to do something about it right away. Because when your life energy depletes more and more, as your power level goes down, you will become physically ill. When our power level is down sufficiently, we die.

Power—its use, its abuse.

Many people abuse power. They use power in the wrong way. They use power to dominate others. Ultimately when you do this, you lose it. They use power to destroy others, to keep others from becoming more powerful because they fear that they will lose something—an element of control.

You see, you can take power from others; you can steal it. Oh, it's not a very high-grade power, that's for sure, but you can steal power.

Just as somebody can work very hard for their money and you could go in and break into their house and take it away and they won't have it. So you can steal power.

You can drain power from others. That power will take you into limited spheres of attention. It will give you a certain amount of access to a better life, a better career, and so on and so forth, but it corrupts the individual.

The person who takes it will never really be happy with those things they gain from it because they've lost their essential balance and innocence. And without innocence, nothing can further, as they say in the *I Ching*.

But suppose you've been imprinted by people who take power from others, which is most, ... almost all human beings in this world.

In other words, I would suggest that a lot of the imprints that you have gained, or imprints that you have gained as you have lived your life, have been imprints of taking power from others—taking power during sexual experiences, taking power from those you associate with in school, taking power from those who you associate with in family relationships, taking power from those you associate with at your job, taking power from people you don't even see physically anymore.

You may have known them years and years ago, but you can still enter into their attention field and drain them.

Most people drain each other.

Or, what's worse is, they're draining you right now, psychically.

To not know about this is not to be protected from it. Innocence does not protect you. Otherwise, the little lamb would never be slaughtered. Purity does not necessarily bring about, by itself, awareness and knowledge and freedom. Otherwise every tree or plant that grows would be totally powerful and totally knowledgeable and totally free because they're completely pure.

In addition to purity, in addition to innocence, we have to have knowledge—the knowledge of good and evil and also a knowledge that transcends good and evil, which is self-awareness.

We have to move beyond the limited parameters that most human beings have and realize that there are thousands and millions of worlds beyond this world—planes of reality.

This is only a small part of the totality. From this island Earth we see only a small fragment of creation and its knowledge. We gain only a limited view of who and what we are.

And our purpose in this life is to gain the view of ourselves. Otherwise, why live? Otherwise, we're total slaves to others who psychically drain us, who abuse us. Or, even if we're somewhat successful at containing this, we just never reach what we could reach.

We never know the miracle of existence.

I'm up at the top of the Continental Divide in a power spot. The sun is going over the mountains now, and there are just a few hazy purple clouds in the background. The sky is fairly clear.

The moment of sunset is the moment when the doorway opens to eternity. That's a very easy time to shift attention. And we're in the twilight of our world. We're in the twilight of this Earth.

The societies and civilizations of human beings will not endure much longer because of their abuses of power. Yet, it's a wonderful time because it's life. We're in eternity, and we're eternal beings.

Free yourself, from happiness and unhappiness. Realize that there's something beyond both and yet, at the same time, revel in your time, revel in this world. You just need to know how.

I'm a teacher. A mystic. I teach people how. And if I can be of some use to you, then I'd be happy to. But you have to work for this knowledge. It won't come easily. It will come.

You have to be the exceptional being who separates themselves from the herd and the fate of the herd. And then you'll find that there are others like yourself of like mind who seek to break the boundaries of human knowledge.

These are the geniuses of our time—those who can look beyond what we call human knowledge and not be so filled with dogma and prejudices to say, "The Earth is, of course, the center of the universe." "How could a man ever fly in a plane?" "How could a woman ever have the right to vote?"

Only a few hundred years ago, these were the beliefs. Well, what are the beliefs today—are they not just as ignorant?

To think that this is the only universe that exists, that the physical creation is all that there is, that we are limited by our bodies, that we are not capable of all knowledge and all intelligence—these are the dogmas of our time.

To not realize that we are affected by everyone around us, that everyone we think about affects us psychically, to not realize that life is a field of power, to not just be happy in our time—to not know these things is criminal, in my opinion.

If you are a sensitive and evolved being, it's simply criminal. To keep yourself in a state of ignorance means that you just add to the negative imprinting that goes on in our world.

Self-discovery, psychic development, occultism, mysticism, self-realization; learning to love and be free, learning to free oneself from the grip of maya, of illusion; learning to live a strategic life so you can create success in everything that you do—economic success, political success, spiritual success—it's all the same.

The principles are the same, and once they're learned, you'll be free. And just to be happy in the moment, to be beyond fear and doubt—what a great gift. It's something that you can gain.

All you need are the tools of knowledge, and then you must apply them intelligently and you can be free. You can be the exception.

But you need to develop a winner's profile, and to do that you need to learn the ways of power.

So what use is power? We are power. We are energy. We are light. We are eternity itself.

But these are only words if you don't have the personal power to unlock the gates of immortality and of mortality. Otherwise you're a victim. Better to be a victor. Better to be beyond victory and defeat and be something else.

Everything depends upon your attention, your awareness. So why not begin now? Why not begin today? Don't be afraid to take a chance, to jump. Because death will swallow you up anyway.

Death is a friend—it encourages us to become aware, to become free. When intelligently applied, the ways of power will free you.

There is something beyond power. It's hard to describe. First, you have to have a great deal of power, even to open up the subject. What's beyond power? The totality of one's being. Some call it nirvana, some enlightenment. We have a higher destiny.

But before you can even scratch the surface of the subject you have to bring your life into order and make it very successful. You need to be happy and free.

You need to be able to see psychically and understand what's going on in the universe, how you're being affected by others, how you affect others, what you really are, what your luminosity is about, how to reorder your luminous fibers, how to clarify and strengthen your mind.

But after you've done those things, which are the basics, then there is something, and we call it freedom. Freedom, knowledge—it's beyond power. Power takes you there, but it's not the end. There is no ending and there is no beginning. That's what makes it so exciting.

Life is not a closed circuit—it's endless. There's always something new. There's always a new adventure.

There's a little bit of snow on some of the mountains up here, even though it's August. A few faint traces. They remind us that winter will come again. In each one of our lives, there is something to remind us that we will be here only a while—the winter will come again. And it encourages us to enjoy these moments in life.

Self-discovery and the study of mysticism should never take you away from being in touch with the most basic things, the most basic happinesses. If you're practicing it correctly, it should cause you to see more beauty in everything, more light.

To be aware—what a wonderful thing. To be awareness itself—a better thing perhaps?

So begin to think about your life. Make lists. Write down the things that give you power. Write the things that take your power away down also. Make lists of people who are close to you, and ask yourself—are your associations raising you to a higher level of attention?

Learn and study the ways of power and be free. Take that field out in the back of your house and plant it in a new way. Find out how if you don't know how.

Learn to overcome the imprinting that you now have and gain a new and higher imprinting that will lead you into the luminous spheres of awareness and cause you to be in charge of your own life, in your own time, in your own being—and will give you freedom.

Don't be afraid.

I and others who have gone through this struggle and who continue, of course, encourage you. We're your friends. You can do it. But don't rely on anyone to do it for you.

Learn what you can from those who have obviously succeeded at anything that you'd like to succeed at, but then implement these things in your own life. And then you can relax and just enjoy the unrivaled fun of the universe.

Self-realization is the last game on earth worth playing. Self-mastery? Yes, but also just enjoyment—enjoyment of the moment and enjoyment of eternity.

So this is Rama up here on top of the Continental Divide at around 11,500 feet, looking at the snow and thinking of death and thinking of rebirth and thinking of all kinds of things. I'm thinking of you!

Good luck. You'll have it.

CHAPTER SEVEN

TRANSCENDENTALISM

The day is August 15th and the location is Walden Pond in Concord, Massachusetts.

The time is 6:30 p.m. I just took a walk around Walden—it's about a 1.8 mile hike—and I stopped for a while at the site of Thoreau's house. They've roped off an area where they discovered the foundation. Occasionally a car is driving back and forth here. It's a sweltering evening. It was in the 90's all day, and the pond is a mecca to swimmers right now. The pond, for those of you who don't know, serves as a beach in the summer, and it has some of the cleanest water in New England.

Our subject tonight is transcendentalism—the awareness of eternity in the present. We ask questions.

What is life? What is its purpose? Does it have a meaning? What is our role in the lila and the cosmic game? How can I find where I belong? Do I belong in this world? Is there a God? If there is a God, what kind of God would make a place like this, where everyone suffers and dies and experiences some transitory happinesses and pleasures?

Transcendentalism answers these and other questions, not so much with verbal answers or with a singular philosophy, but by suggesting that there are layers of reality, and that the average individual only sees one or two of these layers perhaps in an entire lifetime.

But one who is not average, a person who turns their attention inward or who looks with the outward eye but probes beyond the surface, can see that there are other layers or spheres of reality.

The world we see with our senses is a world of appearances—a world of action and interaction, a world of birth and death.

We come into the world and we exist for a while. We learn about our world. We learn the necessary skills to survive for as long as we do. One day, nature appears to overpower us and we leave this world. We die—we cease to exist.

Transcendentalism suggests that we are all part of an "oversoul."

While we have separate finite physical bodies, individual personalities and individual experiences, these are all really a covering. If we could uncover ourselves, if we could remove these layers, then we would see underneath that we're made of something else—that we're made of a light, energy, which the Transcendentalists, of course, referred to as the oversoul.

The oversoul that is in one person is essentially the same oversoul that's in another person—in a tree, in a dog, in a cat, in a planet, in a universe, in an age in the past or the future or the present.

As I'm sitting talking to you, I'm watching a squirrel. I'm sitting here in the Dodge van and I'm watching this cute little guy hop back and forth, apparently oblivious to our technologically oriented civilization. He's out there in his world, a world of trees and nuts and wind and rain and sunshine—completely unaware of the things that we are aware of, and, of course, we are unaware of the things that he is aware of.

So transcendentalism suggests that we are aware of our world, the average person. But we are completely oblivious to a world that may be right next to us. It might be right inside of us—not inside of our bodies per se, but inside of our attention, our consciousness.

Thoreau, Emerson and others were Transcendentalists. And there's a power in the land here in Concord, in Lincoln, in this area—the western Boston suburbs—there's a power here.

There's an inter-dimensional vortex that opens in a variety of places in this area, which leads one to a transcendental reality. This is what we call a place of power.

There are many different places of power around the world. They're invisible openings to other worlds. Not all of them lead to the same worlds.

We find a preponderance of these places in the Himalayas, in the western part of the United States, of course literally in every country of the world there's some. But also, interestingly enough, we find some in the Boston area.

Reality is made up of rooms. God has a living room. God has a bedroom. God has a kitchen, perhaps a playroom. The universe is made up of countless rooms. They're all over. These rooms are levels or planes of awareness.

We normally think that we're in a particular awareness and that our experiences have little or nothing to do with the level of awareness that we're in. For example, we would say that my perception ... the perceptions that you're having, are largely based upon your individualized experiences, your life history, the kind of education that you had, the people who brought you up, the kind of day you had today and so on—never realizing that all of our experiences, our life experiences are really shaped by something far, far different than our simple history.

Our life experiences are shaped by attention, by awareness. Just as we can walk into a very beautiful room or perhaps into a room that's dirty or perhaps into a room that's barren, so there are awarenesses in the universe, and we enter into a particular awareness for a period of time.

While we are in that awareness field, it so colors our seeing of the world and of the universe.

Let me explain what I mean. Let's say, for example, that we see physically, in this world, through the eyes. OK, the eyes present a definite image to us of perception, of reality, of trees, cars, people, houses, experiences. The eyes, though, definitely color our experience.

Suppose we had a different organ of perception. Suppose we couldn't see, and we could just touch. Then we would see and feel—we would touch, rather, and in our touching we would apprehend and get a certain idea of what things were like, which would be far different than seeing, right? So each sense shows us a different side of what is. However, if we just had one sense, we might not get a complete picture.

Well, life is like that. We see a certain side of something and we suppose that that's all that is—because we have nothing to suggest to us that there's a whole different way to perceive something. There is, of course.

The initial step that a person must make in transcendentalism is to come to realize that the perceptions that they're having at this time are not so much created by choice as by a field of attention, a room that we've walked in.

In other words, we're very happy, we're bright, we're in a good mood, and we walk into a room that's kind of dirty—it's got a lot of rubbish around it, the curtains are old, the couch is faded and maybe a lot of unhappy people have been there and we can feel their energy. The room just does not feel perky and happy at all.

When we sit in that room over a period of time, we will begin to feel those feelings—they'll begin to saturate our consciousness and that original happy mood that we had will begin to mutate a little bit, it will begin to transform, transmogrify, and we will begin to absorb some of those feelings, and soon those feelings will take a place in our being. While we might have been very happy or perky, suddenly we'll find ourselves getting a little bit discouraged.

Naturally, we will attribute that feeling, or those feelings and the thoughts that would generate from those feelings. So for example, if you're feeling discouraged, a project you might have been very jazzed about and excited about might now seem difficult or impossible. While it seemed relatively easy when you were in a more open and enthusiastic state, now you might not even do it.

Choices we might make, feelings we might have, a whole list of activities in our life may or may not occur according to the attention fields that we're in. In other words, our own volition is not ultimately important, but it's the sphere of attention that colors all of our perceptions.

Well, the Earth consists of a variety of different spheres of attention. Each physical location has one or more different spheres of attention.

Transcendentalism seeks to see the individual sphere of attention and to note it as a part of reality, as a part of creation. That is to say, we can see that—well, OK, this is one part of life or God, this is another part of life or God, this is another part of life or God. But then there's something that is beyond all of these individualized spheres of attention which, you might say, is their authority.

It is the kind of divine ground that they come forth from. And that's what we would refer to as "transcendental"—that is to say, not limited to any singular interpretation, not limited to the physical world but not necessarily excluding the physical.

So a transcendental experience is not necessarily something that is strictly out of this world and has no contextual reality to it. But a transcendental experience would be something that appears to be while it is not.

It could be an experience of looking at a tree, looking at a flower, looking at a bumblebee and having a sense of its eternality—seeing beyond its simple physical form; seeing the universe within it, seeing, in other words, that other perception, that divine ground—that endless reality which it comes forth from and sustains it and transmutes it—as a solid part of that reality.

In other words, we're all eternal.

We don't begin and we don't end. We have always been and we will always be, but we take on varying forms in the universe. We are consciousness. We are awareness or attention. And we adopt these varying forms from lifetime to lifetime, from dream to dream.

In this lifetime you're in a particular form and your form is shaped by your attention and your attention is shaped, of course, by physical locality; by the awareness net of the people around you; naturally by conditioning, past experiences, descriptions of the world that others have handed you, and so on and so forth.

Transcendentalism suggests that our perception of ourselves is really incomplete; it's inaccurate.

What we need to do is redefine ourselves. And this redefinition comes through a type of meditative activity in which we seek to quiet our lives and our mind and reflect, just as a mirror reflects. A mirror is not an image in itself, but it's a reflector of images.

So our attention can reflect eternity, different aspects of it. If I go down to Walden Pond and I look into the water, during the day I can see the reflection of the sky and the clouds above. At night, naturally, if it's a clear night, I can see the reflection of the sky and the clouds above. At night, if it's a clear night, I can see the stars.

So it reflects, yet it is something itself. It's water. Water will take any shape we assign it to. If we put it in a round cup it will become round; if we put it in a square, it will become square. So consciousness is the same.

Consciousness or attention—our awareness—will change form. It's very adaptable. It will assume the shape it's projected into. If it's projected into a human world, in a human body, it will assume the shape for a while, until it leaves this shape, in which case it will transmute into something else.

But it's also a reflector. We reflect the universe around us as the universe around us reflects the world within us. The world within us reflects eternity.

It's hard sometimes to understand why we do what we do. It's hard sometimes to understand why we feel what we feel. But if you would try to become less attached to the doings and feelings in your life and instead consider the world around you more.

An essential step in becoming a good reflector is in Zen what they call "polishing the mirror." In order to reflect well, the mirror has to be clearly polished—there can't be any dust on the mirror.

Transcendentalism has a lot to do with clearing the mirror of the self. And if the mirror is spotless, of course, we will reflect diverse forms of eternity, which is what we call enlightenment.

Enlightenment is not so much a particular state or condition or actualization. It's not something that's reached or achieved, but it's rather the absence of self in individualized form. There's no more dust on the mirror.

The mirror has broken, as a matter of fact, and it's thousands of tiny little pieces, each one that reflects a different part of the universe. And we can't say that one part is more mirror than another, one part is the dominant part and the other is subservient, because all the pieces are about the same size.

We can stand back and say that they're all part of the whole. They're all the mirror. We can look at each one and see that each one reflects something a little bit different, and we could say that they're all individual. Both would be correct ways of assessing the mirror, the broken mirror, or the mirror of the self.

Thoreau spent two years out here on Walden Pond. He spent two years of his life, as he put it himself, coming to confront nature. He wanted to live with the bare essentials of life—build his own house, grow beans out back, cut his own wood, see how much of his food he could obtain just through the work of his own hands, because he felt civilization was already in a heavy decline in the United States.

This, of course, was around the 1800s, and he wanted to get back to the source and he felt his interaction with nature would help him to achieve that goal.

Nature for Thoreau was a touchstone to a higher reality. In nature, in the woods, and in the ecological balance we see reflected in nature and in the woods, he found suggestions of immortality.

As I'm sitting here the wind is rising. I can hear the birds calling. Occasionally a car starts. Some weary bathers leave the area, a little bit sunburned, cool and wet.

I think Thoreau would have been—old Henry would have been very surprised to see hundreds and hundreds of people flocking to swim in his Walden. But when they swim there, whether they know it or not, something happens to them.

There's a vortex of energy at the bottom of the pond. That's where the inter-dimensional opening is. And as people swim in old Walden Pond, it renews them, it soothes them.

It's a little bit like the pool in "Cocoon," I suppose—any power spot is.

Like all power spots, it needs to be treated with respect, because when you go to a power spot and you think negative or depressing thoughts, they tend to grow stronger. Whereas if you think more positive, happier thoughts, they tend to increase in strength. And of course, if you don't think at all, you move into very transcendental states of awareness.

Thoreau wished to live, he said, with nature because he wanted to confront the essential facts of existence. He felt that by cutting his life into absolute simplicity, nature itself would teach him things about life and the world. And of course, the way his sentence runs, is that he said that he wished, upon coming to his death someday, to die knowing that he had really lived.

So his experiences at Walden, the two years in which he greeted nature in solitude and friends and all the things we read about in *Walden,* are a time of true living for him, and I think we can, of course, ask ourselves the same question—have you really lived?

If you were to die tonight or tomorrow, have you done what you came here to do? And if you have not, why not? And why not get about it—because we never know how much time we have.

Then you may take the view that all experience is transitory and passing and it really doesn't matter what you do, and I would tend to agree with you. But I would also tend to agree with the person that says that everything does matter completely—because both are just ways of talking, ways of beating around the bush.

The essential fact remains—are you living the type of life that you would like to? If not, why not? Naturally it takes courage to step beyond the crowd. Thoreau reflected this courage in his lifestyle at Walden. Of course he reflected this courage in his *Essay On Civil Disobedience* and when he refused to pay the local tax and got put in jail for a night until he got bailed out.

Each of us refuses to pay the local tax in our own way. The taxes of this world are much too high—not so much the governmental taxes but the excise taxes upon living energy, upon beingness.

It's essential to make a stand at some point. Winning and losing—these are ideas. But you have to sum up the complete totality of your power and bring it up into your being because otherwise, the world of people and things will wear you down.

Everyone seems to have their idea of who you should be and what you should be doing. You even have your own ideas, and they're not necessarily even your own ideas. What can you do?

Well, the most important thing, obviously, is to develop the sense of balance in your life and a sense of happiness—a reverence for life, a sensitivity just for the state of beingness that we find ourselves in in this world.

It's equally important to love. To love is not as complicated as it sounds, so love deeply. Love is the recognition of the infinite in someone else. And when you love someone, that infinite reality unfolds itself to you.

Giving is an essential part of all existence. Life gives itself to us. We give ourselves to life. Giving creates a sense of joy and purposefulness that frees us from what could otherwise be an unpleasant experience in this thing that we call life.

Giving elevates us above the ego and the simplistic desires that are basically insatiable and just run round and round and round us. It gives us a feeling of ... it is a balance!

And it creates a sense of hope. Because when we give, we become lighter, we become freer and we become happier—when we give, of course, unconditionally, without any strings attached.

What is the meaning and purpose of life? Well, there isn't really a singular meaning and purpose to life. There are as many meanings and purposes as there are people. And the meaning and purpose of your life will change as you shift.

The trick is to be aware of all you can be—to try to be as conscious as possible, not just of the things in your immediate surroundings or your physical environment or the people that you know or the magazines that you might read or the books that you might study. These are things to be conscious of.

But try more and more to peel back that layer between yourself and the transcendental reality. Try and look more deeply into things.

As you're sitting reading, or you're walking through the woods or whatever you may be doing, have the sense that you are not only walking through the woods on this Earth, but you are walking through the woods of eternity.

When you talk to someone, don't simply feel that you're talking to another individualized being, but try to have the sense that you are talking to a being that is infinitely old, that's always been, that knows all things—not simply the person in front of you, but there's another being there too.

Feel that when you walk through the world, you're walking through thousands and millions of worlds. This physical world we see in front of us and around us is only a tiny suggestion of what is. The miracle of life and perception is endless.

We ourselves are that miracle. Our very existence, our ability to live as conscious beings, perceivers of attention, suggests life.

The most amazing thing there is, is life.

There's truth in just about everything. There's a lot of truth in the mirror. A lot of truth in the people you love. A lot of truth, of course, in the things that you love. Love is, really, I think, the best way to truth. There are many ways, but I definitely prefer love (just rolling down the window here to let a little air in; it's pretty hot here.)

Why love? Well, to begin with, love is just a lot of fun. And if you don't live with love, then all you do is feel your body all the time. You feel its desires, its pains, and so on. It's pretty dull, a pretty slow way to perceive. Love is a much faster way to process.

We live in an era, naturally, where love is a joke. Really, practically no one loves anymore—because everyone is just so jaded. By the age of three you've seen and done everything you can possibly do [Rama laughs]—by nine you've done it five times, right?

There just doesn't seem to be a whole lot of innocence around, but yes, there is. Remember, nothing is as it appears to be. You're just seeing one part of the movie of creation right now. You're in a particular field of attention where love is difficult to find, where truth seems hidden, where frustration is a part of your daily activity.

But just on the other side of attention there's another field of consciousness, another room you can walk into. When you walk into that room, everything changes.

We are the places that we go. We are the people that we meet. We are the things that we experience and yet, there's something deeper within us—an experiencer—someone who's watching all of this, the observer.

And yet we are the things we observe. We are the life in the trees. We are the sound of the wind.

The wind is shifting. More and more people are leaving the pond. The sun is just beginning to set. And when the sun sets, of course, it's easier to feel eternity.

During that in-between time—sunrise, sunset—there are moments of transition when nothing is completely fixed and solid. Perception shifts, and if you're attuned you can shift with it.

There aren't as many people in the world as we like to think there are. I say that because the people that we see around us appear to be different, but they're really just about the same. They think the same thoughts, wear the same clothes, go to the same schools, buy the same cars, fight the same battles. It's really not a lot of difference. There are very few people in this world.

Yet, occasionally, the individualist will come along—someone who marches to the beat of a different conga drum, someone who looks more deeply, who drinks of the waters of life more completely, who asks more questions, who is more silent, who loves more deeply, who's a better friend.

You may be one of those beings.

There isn't a beginning or there isn't an ending. Life is a continuum. It's a circle. We go round and round and round. First we see one side of the circle, then the other, then the next, then the next. Then we find ourselves back at the beginning.

Yet each time we complete a circuit of the circle, something changes—we do. We are not the same person or being that was back at the beginning of the circle when we started. Therefore the circle itself changes—its meaning changes, its definition changes.

Holiness is something that is best reserved for one's own heart. I think it's very important to protect and preserve your experiences in higher attention. We treat them too commonly, and they're much, much too special. It's best to be silent about the things that you see in life that really matter because otherwise, either people will deride them and laugh at them, or they'll lose a certain element of power that they have when you share them.

On the one hand, it's kind of like throwing your pearls before swine. On the other hand, there's just something lost in the transmission. There's a certain amount of power and energy that we have in our experience—when we have a metaphysical journey, a meditation—and that power tends to fade when we share it with someone because there's only so much of it. When we share it, we are giving it away.

I'm a great believer in the positive power of nature. While it's possible to sit in the meditation hall and meditate and conduct spiritual conversations with others and to read books of transcendental philosophy, I think the really exciting things happen when we go out for a walk by ourselves in the woods. And something in nature purifies us. The experience that we have as we walk and look at trees and leaves, or snow, whatever the condition of the weather may be, washes us.

We live too much inside. We live inside and we have square thoughts and square ideas because we live in square houses.

Our lives are colored by our environment. Our attention fields are colored by it. When we go out and we walk around in the wilds of nature and we tromp down leaves and walk down paths or maybe walk a place no person has ever been, an aliveness comes into our being, a sense of wellness, a sense of the simple and terrific beauty of the Earth.

Nature. Enjoy it on the planet Earth while it lasts.

There are different types of meditation. There are of course types of meditations where we sit and still our thoughts, but there's a type of meditation that involves just walking.

Nature will soothe us, nature will still the thoughts.

Now, some teachers, of course, have said, "Well, walking in nature is sort of like taking a prescription drug. Walking in nature will not last. We take a prescription drug and it takes care of the symptoms, but it doesn't go to the root cause of the matter."

What they're saying is that, yes, your thoughts do stop to a certain extent when you are exposed to nature and you do the walking in the woods. But it's not the same as when you learn to formally meditate and you can control your thoughts in any situation and in any environment.

Of course, I would agree with that, but at the same time, I think there's nothing wrong with prescription drugs once in a while. Because our thoughts do stop and we do reduce the environmental pollution within the mind when we are in nature.

Nature soothes us. Nature heals us—and something more. The woods are a place of power. Any woods that are still surviving on this planet, those are powerful areas to have kept themselves free from the encroachment of the industrial societies of our Earth.

And I think it's a very important thing for anyone who seeks the transcendental experience to spend a few hours every other day in nature, just out there tromping around. That's what old Henry David Thoreau used to do. He called it "sauntering." He would walk for hour after hour in the woods.

Whether you walk or jog or hop or whatever it is you do, your time spent in nature—in addition to your meditation, in addition to your sort of philosophical thoughts and in addition to having a wonderful sense of humor about yourself in your life—will enable you to loosen up a little bit and to feel the oversoul, to feel those different layers of consciousness and attention.

In *Walden,* Thoreau has a chapter of his book about solitude. And he asserts, essentially, that solitude is—I'm rolling up the window because it's getting a little noisy out there—that solitude is totally important, that solitude is where we find ourselves in a unique way.

Who could not agree with such a statement?

Walking in the woods, it's easier to be alone. In the streets of the city, just the volume and broadcast basis of the thought forms that emanate from human beings are so strong. But the trees actually act as a field of absorption, all that green—or the mountains or the deserts or wherever human beings are sparse.

Nature actually absorbs a certain amount of the thought energy that human beings generate, so you can have a little peace of mind.

The Earth renews itself constantly. The green belt of the Earth generates oxygen for living beings to breathe. Without the green world, of course, none of us would be here. The Earth cleanses itself through rain. It shifts its attention through earthquakes, creates new continents, dissolves old continents.

The Earth is alive. We are alive.

Our bodies are constantly changing. We're breathing, transpiring, creating cells, cells are dying. We're a universe and our awareness is limitless. It's only limited by what we think. What we think is what we become, but we are not the thoughts. We are the space in between the thoughts. We are the silent observer that watches all of this without condemnation, without approval and sees something that the eye, the physical eye, can't see.

Our friend, which is eternity.

It's nice to have a relationship with eternity in which you see eternity as your friend, not as your opponent. Nature is not something to conquer but something to learn from or to merge with or to join and be part of—to dance with, celebrate.

To celebrate life is a fine thing. And it really doesn't require a party, just yourself and your good wishes towards the universe.

Take yourself on out for a walk, get out of your problems and your turmoil and go walking. Go saunter down into the woods, walk along a path or a quiet lane or through a park.

Send your good wishes to the universe. Spread your good will everywhere, and you'll find that your life will transform, your body will be energized, hope will fill your being. Because you are now moving into a different field of attention.

You're reshaping reality by the structure of your thoughts.

Nothing is neither good nor bad, only thinking makes it so. So says Shakespeare. And I would say, "Nothing is — unless we think it."

If we don't think, then what is there? Eternity—in all of its countless, endless forms and its formlessness. Nirvana, that which cannot be described.

So a walk in the woods can reveal many things, and it is a good time to practice transcendentalism.

Look at a tree and realize it's not just a tree—its roots may go into the ground but it may also go into other worlds, other eternities. It reaches for the sky in the same way that we reach for light. It bends as the light shifts; its leaves grow to it. So we bend and we shift to the light, we seekers of the transcendental experience.

Go to the beach and look out at the ocean and just stare. Not at any fixed horizon in this world, but at the endless horizon that beckons us all.

Who knows what we may discover today, let alone tomorrow or the next day—what realization we'll come to? Those who think that they've seen and experienced life are fools. There's no end to life. They've only scratched the surface. They've only seen the extent to which their thoughts can carry them.

Beyond thoughts is no mind. Beyond no mind is existence itself.

Thoughts also are a reflection of eternity. Just as the physical things in this world are part of life and part of God, so are thoughts. And when a person is obsessed with thoughts or concerns of this world, we can't say they're any less in God than someone else who is not.

We can't say that the enlightened person or being is more God than someone else is because everything is God—varying and shifting gradients and forms of God, of eternity, of eternal truth.

Transcendentalism sees that each one of us is eternity. We are eternal travelers, eternal journeyers.

So here I am at Walden, in the parking lot, sitting here as the hour is growing later, talking with you when I suppose I should be out doing things—however, the things never seem to matter too much. I do them sometimes because they are there to do, and sometimes I seek to avoid them and spend my time in the woods, walking about, remembering and forgetting who I am and what I'm not and what I might be—having adventures by myself, with myself and sometimes without myself. And I suggest that you do the same.

Renew your friendship with nature. Transcendentalism flourishes in nature; it flourishes in the city, it's true. But we've seen the cities and spent so much time there. It's time now for nature. It's time to go on the road and journey into the innermost recesses of being.

Don't be afraid of your pains and your fears—better to have your pains and fears out here where you can live, than sitting in a little room or a little apartment or a condominium all by yourself.

Nature beckons us. The transcendental adventure calls us forth.

Nature is the endless reflective pattern of existence in eternity.

As I sit here watching the leaves and watching their patterns outside of the windows of my truck here, I'm reminded of so many things I've seen in other planes and in other worlds.

I see all kinds of beings, of course, zipping in and out of the forest here. Non-physical beings moving around—living in their worlds and their spectrums, as physical beings live in their worlds and their spectrums, as beings like myself live in-between worlds.

Each of us seeks to find a balance, a place where we belong. The importance is not of being earnest or rich or famous. The importance is finding that still point, that balancing point that's within your own heart.

And as you love and give yourself over to whatever it is you are, as we relent and stop fighting the process of our own becoming and being, and we accept our limitations and we embrace them and we accept the limitless and embrace that, we come to a wonderful sense of what it is to be in this world—to be alive, to be eternal.

We realize our foolishness with life, and we enjoy its gifts while it lasts.

Transcendentalism is ultimately a reflection of itself. It's ourselves looking into the mirror of existence. We peer more and more deeply. Mirror, mirror, on the wall, which is the fairest reality of them all? Well, it's the one that we're seeing at any given moment. And then that moment will change and another mirage will fade and another will appear and another will fade.

There really isn't a purpose to it—it's just a wonderful show that we can engage in happily or unhappily, in which we can be losers or winners, in which we can suffer or know joy, in which we can have knowledge or be fools.

And in one life or another we play all of those parts, and hopefully play them well.

We're all actors and actresses on the great stage of life, and what really matters is not the role we play, but that we play it well—that we play it perfectly, impeccably. So in this life, if you seek the transcendental, then that's the role that you should play well.

You should meditate deeply, give completely and be awed by all of life. Not become jaded or disillusioned because others may be jaded and disillusioned, but instead just rejoice in the moment of being, in the moment of stillness or in the time of activity. One should be of good cheer and be hopeful. Why not?

Eternity is your friend. You need to feel it all the time—it's just your friend. It's always with you. You are of it and it is of you. You can't be separated from eternity.

It is your domain, as you are its puppet. It is your puppet, as it is your domain. As they say in some of the Eastern spiritual books, "I am thine, thou art mine."

So transcendentalism is the spirit of eternity. It's the spirit of well wishing, of seeing beyond the surface.

Henry Thoreau came out here to look in Walden Pond and he saw the stars like dust reflected in it.

And yet Walden had its own depths, and he saw the depths of his own soul to some extent out here—in this beautiful power place, on this wonderful planet, in this fantastic galaxy, in this endless creation.

So seek more deeply. Meditate more quietly. And walk in the woods! Get out there and hike a little bit and look at eternity and let it look at you. And maybe life will work out pretty well. You won't know till you get out here, what you're missing.

So this is "so long" from Rama, in the transcendental reality with lots of beings in and around the truck at Walden Pond, on the 15th of August.

Also by the Author

BOOKS

Surfing the Himalayas

Snowboarding to Nirvana

Lifetimes: True Accounts of Reincarnation

Total Relaxation: The Complete Program for
Overcoming Stress, Tension, Worry, and Fatigue

The Bridge Is Flowing But The River Is Not

The Lakshmi Series

The Wheel of Dharma

Insights: Talks On The Nature of Existence

Rama Live In LA

Talks and Workshops

The Last Incarnation

A Workshop With Rama

On The Road With Rama

Psychic Development

Zen Tapes

Tantric Buddhism

The Enlightenment Cycle

Insights: Tantric Buddhist
Reflections on Life

MUSIC

Atlantis Rising

Breathless

Canyons of Light

Cayman Blue

Ecstasy

Enlightenment

Light Saber

Mandala of Light

Mystery School

Occult Dancer

Retrograde Planet

Samadhi

Samurai

Surfing the Himalayas

Tantra (2 vols)

Techno Zen Master

Urban Destruction

Zen Master

On the Road With Rama

Published 2021 by Living Flow
www.livingflow.com
Boulder, CO 80302 USA

Paperback ISBN 978-1-947811-37-9
Ebook . . . ISBN 978-1-947811-38-6

Publisher's Code r026-v11

Cover art & design by Meg Popovic
Interior dragon art by Janis Wilkins
Back cover photo by Greg Gorman

147

Made in United States
North Haven, CT
08 November 2024